New ways in discipline

New ways in discipline

YOU AND YOUR CHILD TODAY

by *Dorothy Walter Baruch*

illustrations by Lois Fisher

Whittlesey House

McGRAW-HILL BOOK COMPANY, INC · New York · London · Toronto

NEW WAYS IN DISCIPLINE

SECOND PRINTING

PUBLISHED BY WHITTLESEY HOUSE

A DIVISION OF THE McGRAW-HILL BOOK COMPANY, INC.

Printed in the United States of America

71712
3-50

Preface

Parents, children and teachers have come to me for many years, formerly when I was director of the laboratory school at Broadoaks School of Education, Whittier College, and more recently in private practice as a consulting psychologist. Throughout the years I have noticed that regardless of the age of a child, parents and teachers alike are more concerned with *discipline* than with any other topic.

And this is as it should be.

For, on the shoulders of parents and teachers falls the major task of imparting to children the ways of our difficult culture. It is their privilege and their responsibility to make civilized people out of little hellions and little angels alike.

The parent starts the child out in life. Later, parent and teacher share the task. Too often, the sharing is in name only. The parent goes one way, the teacher another. Even in their psychological orientation, they are miles apart.

This makes obvious difficulties for the child. Parents and teachers need not only to know each other but to pool knowledge and information. Even more important, they need to have some common, basic understandings of the psychological aspects governing wholesome discipline today.

When a child first goes to school, he takes with him all the years that have gone before. Into kindergarten, he takes his infancy and his toddling days. When he enters high school, he carries within all the experiences he has had in other grades

v

as well as at home. And so, the teacher and the parent both should know something of the years that have gone before. They should know of the child's emotional needs and requirements and of the kind of regimen which would have furthered his best adjustments at each period in his life. For, with such common backgrounds, teachers and parents together can make up in the present for mistakes that have occurred in the past. With such common backgrounds the various adults can pool effort and skills to make the future a happier one for both them and the child.

One other person enters the scene all along. This is the doctor. Parents look to him for help and advice. Teachers similarly go to him as a source of wisdom. Therefore it will be beneficial if he, too, can acquire similar orientation and insights into the psychological management of children to add to his store of knowledge on the physical side.

It is to these three groups of people—parents, teachers and doctors—that the present book is addressed in the hope that it may bring to them some of the answers they are seeking in helping children acquire new strengths to meet a new world.

DOROTHY WALTER BARUCH

Of my indebtedness

As one works professionally over the years directly with parents and children and as one works also with teachers, social workers and others, trying to reach understandings and insights—one's practice, philosophy and ideas become something of an amalgam of rare and precious materials gathered from all ends of the earth. These mingle with what one has discovered from explorations on one's own.

Were I to quote all the sources of knowledge and inspiration that have contributed to this book, the bibliography would be massive and the names legion. Many friends and colleagues will come across their ideas on these pages. As they do, they will know how grateful I am to them for having shared these with me in writings or in conversations.

Some things need specific mention:

Although this book does not assume a nondirective approach to child management, I am indebted to Carl Rogers for the term "reflection," which so appropriately describes an important and useful technique . . .

For much of the normative material in the earlier years I am indebted to Arnold Gesell and his collaborators at Yale, and for the basic material on the puberal period to such workers as Herbert and Lois Stoltz, Harold Jones, Peter Blos, Fritz Redl and Caroline Tryon . . .

For the material on the regimen of infancy including the question of rooming-in and self-demand schedules to people like Edith

Jackson, Benjamin Spock, C. A. Aldrich, John Dorsey, John C. Montgomery, F. P. Simsarian and others who have pioneered in the field . . .

Recent books and articles that have come my way and have contributed to earlier concepts on the dynamics and handling of childhood aggression include titles by David M. Levy, Lawrence Kubie, Anna Freud, Margaret Mead, Lauretta Bender, S. R. Slavson, Lawrence K. Frank, and many, many more . . .

Samuel Lewis is the dentist who did the research on thumb-sucking referred to in Chapter 7; Marbry and Allen Edwards are the designers and builders of the Baby Haven, which they adapted from the "Box" invented by B. F. Skinner; Evelyn Feltenstein and her colleagues at the Downtown Community School in New York were good enough to compile and contribute some of their ideas; Emily Pribble Gillies, who wrote a moving article called "Crosses and Knives" in *Childhood Education*, May, 1946, is quoted in Chapter 14 from a paper she turned in when she was at one and the same time a student of mine and a most gifted teacher in the Los Angeles city schools. Some of the other quotations in the same chapter are from a report sent to the International Congress on Mental Health held in London, August, 1948. They were contributed variously by Alice and Paul Bohem, Amy Mathews, Dorothy Johnson, Belle Dubnoff, Doris Chabot and Evelyn Schechter, all teachers in Los Angeles public schools. The story about "Florence" in Chapter 4 is from an article of mine that appeared in *Parents' Magazine*, October, 1947. Parts of Chapter 6 appeared as an article in *Vogue*, March 15, 1949; parts of Chapters 6 and 15 in *Parents' Magazine*, March and April, 1949, respectively; and parts of Chapter 14 in *Childhood Education*, March, 1949 . . .

I am grateful to Lenore Gillies, who not only typed the manuscript with loving care but who offered valuable suggestions out of her own experience as a mother . . .

Norman Nixon was the first of my friends to go over the manuscript and to view it from the vantage point of pediatric psychiatry. I am immeasurably grateful to him for his warm and generous evaluation and for his thoughtful and wise suggestions . . .

Especially am I grateful to Hyman Miller, my husband, whose patience never fluctuated even in the wee hours when I would read newly written pages for his comments. His wide background of both medical and psychological knowledge and his critical and kindly appraisal stimulated, challenged and invigorated my efforts all along . . .

Most particularly am I grateful to the many parents and children who shared of their deepest and innermost feelings and gave me permission to use them . . .

None of these people are responsible for any errors I may have committed in citing them. But each and every one of them is responsible—as are many others—for whatever authenticity and strength and value lie in this book.

To HY
who helped me make this book helpful

In brief

                                                                xi

PART THREE
WHAT YOU CAN DO IN TIMES OF PEACE
TO REDUCE TIMES OF STRESS

PART FOUR
MOVING AHEAD

New ways in discipline

1. Preview: To spank or not to spank?

The modern parents' dilemma

With many different voices and in many different ways, parents from all parts of the land are asking one particular question. Although they are concerned with various phases of bringing up their children, this one question stands at the top of the list: *What shall we do about disciplining our children?* Teachers are echoing the question: *How shall we discipline these same children in school?*

Says one mother, "Had I lived earlier, it would have been so much easier. Back in the teeming twenties I could have spanked my youngster without a single qualm. If he'd turned the jet on the gas stove I'd have reached for the ruler and rapped his knuckles soundly, saying to myself, *There! I've taught him not to touch the stove any more.* Then I would have smirked with satisfaction, thinking to myself, *Now when he looks at the jet and is tempted to turn it, his mind will say to him, 'Touching it brings a ruler down on me. The ruler will hurt me. So better not!'*

"If I'd lived about twenty-five years ago I wouldn't have worried about what such a method of discipline might do to him and me—to our relationship. I wouldn't have stopped to think that when he looked at the gas jet, his mind might sound

1

another note entirely. It might say to him, 'Touching the jet brings mother down on me. She hurts me. I'd better turn it on fast before she comes to stop me. She's an old horrid thing! She always spoils my fun.'

"What has he learned? To fear the gas jet? No! He's learned to fear his mother!"

In our times, more it seems than ever before, parents are like travelers in a land where they can no longer trust the old signposts and where they can't quite make out the lettering on the new. When they can discover no clear new direction, they hark back to the old and familiar. But they find with dismay that they have somehow lost confidence in it. And they try with a false kind of bravado to cover the feeling of being lost.

YOU DON'T WANT TO SPOIL HIM

A broad-shouldered, stalwart father argued aggressively, "There's one thing I'll tell *you*. There's nothing like a good old-fashioned spanking every once in a while."

He was met with a nod and an understanding answer, "You believe that spanking is necessary."

At this he broke into a boyish grin and confided, "It's a necessary *evil!* I guess because I don't know anything better to do."

As is true of many parents, he had an uneasy feeling that the old rules of disciplining were not what he believed in. And yet he clung to them because he had nothing to take their place. Actually, he was lost and confused. His confidence in the old directions was gone and he had not yet found new ones.

Another father voices the same dilemma. "Look," he says, "I've got two kids and if they have to grow up as scared of me as I was of my dad and as scared of themselves as I've always been, I'd go out and shoot myself fast. And yet I don't want my children to be unruly. I've got to see that they get some

2

disciplining. Tell me, what the heck am I supposed to do?"

Far too often parents feel that discipline is an EITHER-OR proposition, that it leads either to one extreme or the other. On one side, they have visions of a spoiled-brat horror—a nasty, demanding, unruly and obnoxious child. On the other

To spank or not to spank?

hand, they see a person who has had all the initiative and spontaneity knocked out of him, who stands with a hangdog, cowed air. They want neither.

The resulting confusion is common. It arouses many feelings of uncertainty and countless querulous queries. One parent asks, "How about playing with my baby? Is it all right or will I spoil him? Should I pick him up or just let him lie

3

and cry it out?" . . . Another wonders, "How about my still unsteady walker? Shan't I insist on his being clean when he eats?" . . . Still another ponders weightily on the wild adolescent under his wing. "Ye gods, when my daughter brings home a flock of lipsticked sophisticates and supercondescending youths who make shambles of the house, am I supposed to slink out and retire in bedroom slippers, or should I insist that cigarette butts and burns are simply not the order of the day?"

"When the yapping cowboys start lassoing the lamps in the library and the masked bandits begin shooting at the pursuing police, what on earth am I supposed to do?"

In the schools, teachers have much the same problems. "Should you line children up in military rank and file and yell at them or slap them down? Or should you let them raise the roof, yip like hyenas and overflow through every window and door?"

"What shall we say?" "What shall we do?"

And so it goes, over and over, in continuous refrain.

DISCIPLINE IS ESSENTIAL!

We realize today that discipline is essential. Every child needs leadership and guidance. The idea of giving him complete freedom and license is recognized for what it is—a grave misconception. It just isn't fair. It places too much responsibility on shoulders that are not strong enough to carry it. A child has neither the background nor knowledge, neither the wisdom nor judgment. The weight of the responsibility can crush him. He is called upon to do more than he is able so he loses confidence in himself. He feels, "I'm expected to handle all this on my own but I can't; it's too big. I'm not man enough to do it. I'm just no good."

Too much discipline does practically the same thing as too little discipline. Too much discipline also gives the child a feeling of failure. He cannot live up to *all* the things the

4

adults expect of him. Again he feels that the burden is too heavy to bear.

In its derivation, the term "discipline" has to do with following a leader. The disciples of Christ were followers of Jesus. The disciples of Hitler were his followers.

But the quality of leadership in these two instances had very different effects on the motives and actions of the followers. The leader himself, the quality of his being and of his essential personality enter into the picture as does also the relationship between the leader and the led.

Parents can lead by either the Whip or the Word. So also can teachers. But the Word demands much more of sharing, of living together. It calls on us and the child for building mutual understandings and confidence.

Fortunately, discipline need not be synonymous with dictatorship or castigation. Even though punishment does sometimes seem the only way out, even though rules and regulations are necessary and do have a definite place, there is still another part to discipline that has been too greatly neglected. Through attention to this other part, much of the punitive, demanding, dictatorial part can be eliminated so that both children and adults find far more peace.

THE REASON WHY DISCIPLINE DOESN'T WORK

An extremely important reason why discipline fails is that a child's "badness" has two parts to it, and we deal only with one part and leave the other out entirely.

A child ACTS NAUGHTY. That's one part of the problem. A child FEELS NAUGHTY. That's the other part. He does mean things because he has mean feelings inside him. His feelings are the *cause;* his actions are the *result.*

In our ordinary manner of disciplining a child we deal with his actions and ignore his feelings. We say to a teen-ager, for instance, "You've got to be more helpful around the house!" We insist on "more cooperation," but we do not go into the

5

feelings that keep him from cooperating. We say to a six-year-old youngster, "Now be nice to your little sister!" Again, however, we fail to go into the feelings that are making him mean. We keep on and on dealing with actions alone. Seldom if ever do we deal with the feelings that cause children to behave as they do. In our discipline we put all our emphasis on the "bad" actions and do not try to help the child get rid of the "bad" feelings that lie underneath.

We don't intend to ignore the feelings but we've never learned how to handle them. No one has ever taught us. We've never even thought that dealing with a child's feelings constituted a necessary part of discipline. And so we have failed often when failure might not have resulted had we taken feelings into account.

Actually, we need to deal with both feelings and actions. Otherwise, our discipline fails to have the positive and lasting results we want it to have.

> For GOOD DISCIPLINE and GOOD BEHAVIOR
> we must deal with a child's
> FEELINGS as well as his ACTIONS.

This book tells us how.

Ordinarily, when we talk of discipline, we think in terms of what to do at certain moments of stress, as when a child refuses to go to bed or is impertinent or won't come when he is called. We fight our way through the issue and then dismiss the disciplinary measures till the next issue arises. This is another reason why our discipline fails.

What we do to discipline our child should include things we undertake in peaceful moments as well as in troublesome ones.

Fortunately, there are many things that we can do with our children in the course of their daily living from infancy through adolescence which deal with feelings as well as actions and which *prevent* the stress periods in discipline from

6

arising. They *prevent* emotional sores from bursting into sudden eruptions. They also *heal* where the sores have already burst. They *heal* the rawness and hurt. They are both preventives of disciplinary problems and curatives after the problems arise. In short, they possess the psychological value of MAKING DISCIPLINE EASIER. They clear the way for wholesome followship and shape the job of leadership into a much happier thing.

And curiously, since we don't ordinarily associate such a word with discipline, among these procedures we shall find activities which ordinarily are thought of as *play*. They are zestful activities, down to earth, real and tangy. They carry challenge and sometimes creative endeavor, so that in the long run they often prove *fun*.

"When you say *play* and *fun*, do you mean like the good old-fashioned fun of bobbing for apples or stringing popcorn or going on weenie bakes? If so, we've tried it. But things invariably happen that increase the disciplinary problems instead of reducing them! Last Hallowe'en, for instance, after we'd hauled the wooden tub down from the attic and had filled it with water, what did Tommy do but drop the kitten in!

"And as for picnics! We managed to find a babbling brook. But then Betty slipped on a moss-covered rock and shrieked bloody murder and Bobby and Bunny got to fighting over who'd get the biggest cooky and the baby got stung by a bee. But—" wistfully—"next time we may have more fun."

"You hear that fathers and sons should do things together. Well, I took Tad, my seven-year-old, to the football game. He kept jerking my coat and asking, 'Hey, Dad, who's got the ball now?' Finally, to shush him, I got him a hot dog. And then it was—jerk—'Can I have another?' and—jerk—'Another?' until I finally jerked myself out of my stupor and realized I must have bought him ten!

"I told him in no uncertain terms, then, that he couldn't

have more. But would he listen? Not on a bet. The fun really started. Only not the sort I prefer!"

With proper planning and willing spirit the old-fashioned activities can still be invigorating. Yet it isn't with these that we'll deal. For every adult can go back into the storehouse of his own childhood and pull out the most relished bits to freshen up and homogenize for present consumption.

But most parents and teachers have not been equipped to bring into being those *activities which have psychological value in connection with discipline.* It is these, as well as other phases of discipline, that we will explore. We will not only try to see *what makes children "ornery" and "bad";* we will also—and mostly—focus on *what makes them better.* We will go into what grownups can do, what children can do, and what grownups and children can do together *to make discipline easier.*

Incidentally and gladly, we will find in the going that the activities which we discover also enhance mutual rapport and understanding. They cement closeness between adults and children so that they build firmer friendship. Discipline then becomes a matter of fellowship as well as followship. Many blowups are prevented which would bring bitterness and fear and the cowed look in their wake.

The materials required for our new undertakings are not shelves full of games and expensive equipment, but rather the equipment of heart and hand and head that lies within the children's and adults' own power to conjure up. Chief among the things that matter is the adult's eagerness for becoming attuned to how a child feels. The major assets are the ear that listens, the eye that watches, the open mind, and a true, deep and earnest wish to develop sympathy and accord.

Part one

Making discipline easier

2. Stop! look! listen!

DO YOU KNOW YOUR CHILD?

Our ways with children are often strange. Usually, when we want to help a child grow in behavior as he should, we look at what we want him to be like and fail to look at what he *is* like. As one parent aptly put it, "I've been so busy focusing on the regulations that I don't know the person I'm regulating."

When we want a plant to grow, we take pains to understand its nature and nurture. We ask, "What does this plant need? What are its requirements? Will it do better in sun or shade? Does it need a lot of water or a small amount? Much cultivation or little?" If the plant fails to behave as it should, if it does not grow straight and green and gay, we ask, "Where have we neglected to give it what it must have?"

If a child fails to grow in physique as he should, we make similar inquiries. "Are we not feeding him properly? Should he have more vitamins? More milk? A different formula to nourish him?"

If a child fails to grow in behavior as he should, we need to do the same sort of thing. We need to take stock and ask, "What is this child like? What are its requirements? Where are we perhaps overlooking some of its needs?"

But too often we do another sort of thing. We blame the child for failing us; not ourselves for failing him. We heap all kinds of condemnation on his shoulders. "He's bad," we say.

11

"He's terrible." "He's a mess." And then we begin to focus, and we stay focused on how to get him to do what *we* want him to do. We focus so hard on *our* requirements that we disregard *his*.⊙

We focus so hard and furiously on what we want and expect him to do that we lose sight entirely of what he is like. We never get to know him. And so we ignore his requirements. We fail to nourish his needs.

Sis: "Didn't your folks bring you up right?"

"Why don't you do what I want?" yelled an irate mother.

"Because you don't do what I want," her angry child yelled back.

Astonished, she stopped in her tracks and gasped. "What do you mean?"

The answer came swiftly. "I want you to pay attention to me. Then I'll pay attention to you."

"Oh boy!" said the mother thoughtfully later. "Did he say a mouthful!" And so he had.

12

A child must have certain foods to satisfy his bodily needs. He must have proteins, carbohydrates, fats, minerals and vitamins if he is to be physically healthy and well. Otherwise, physical disturbances are apt to arise. Just so must he have certain kinds of nourishment to satisfy his emotional needs. Otherwise, emotional disturbances are apt to arise. As we have indicated, it is these emotional disturbances which lie at the bottom of most of our disciplinary ills.

EMOTIONAL HUNGER LIES AT THE ROOT OF DISCIPLINARY PROBLEMS

What are the emotional foods that every human being must have regardless of age? What are the basic emotional requirements that must come to every small infant, to every growing child, to every adult?

In the first place, there must be *affection* and a lot of it. Real down-to-earth, sincere loving. The kind that carries conviction through body-warmth, through touch, through the good, mellow ring in the voice, through the fond look that says as clearly as words, "I love you for what you are, beyond any nasty thing you might do. I love you because you are you."

Closely allied with being loved should come the sure knowledge of *belonging*, of *being wanted*, the glow of knowing oneself to be part of some bigger whole. *Our* town, *our* school, *our* work, *our* family—all bring the sound of togetherness, of being united with others, not isolated or alone.

Every human being needs also to have the nourishment of *pleasure that comes through his senses*. Color, balanced form and beauty to meet the eye, harmonious sounds to meet the ear. The hearty enjoyment of touch and taste and smell. And finally, the realization that the pleasurable sensations of sex can be right and fine and a part of the spirit as well as of the body.

Everyone must feel that he is capable of *achievement*. He needs to develop the ultimate conviction, strong within him,

13

that he *can* do things, that he is adequate to meet life's demands. He needs also the satisfaction of knowing that he can gain from others *recognition* for what he does.

And most important, each and every one of us must have *acceptance* and *understanding.* We need desperately to be able to share our thoughts and feelings with some one person, or several, who really understands. We long to shed all hypocrisy and pretense and to lay aside defensiveness and affectation. We yearn for the deep relief of knowing that we can be ourselves with honest freedom, secure in knowledge that says, "This person is *with* me. He *accepts* how I feel!"

Too few of us ever have this kind of understanding. And so certain parts of us must stay on guard, fearful of discovery, hurt in the sense of aloneness, and often resentful that no one can see what we really are.

As an individual's basic needs are satisfied, he can develop a sense of his own SELFHOOD. *I am I; and I am somehow a worth-while person. I can relate myself to others with something good to give them. Because I am worth while they will want to relate themselves to me.*

In contrast, if basic needs are unsatisfied, SELFISHNESS replaces the sense of one's own sure and good and fruitful identity. *I'm worth so little I can't take for granted that anyone will like me. I'll have to watch out for and defend myself and clutch for straws and grab with gnawing, hungry greed whatever crumbs I can.*

If any of the basic elements of emotional nourishment are missing, a human being suffers. We, who are already grown, know this. When we feel a lack of love, we become hurt and frightened and often resentful. "You're a brute not to love me. I hate you. I'll make you sorry; you just wait and see."

When we feel a lack of being wanted, we turn touchy and apprehensive and often vindictive. "If you won't have me, I won't have you."

When bodily pleasure has been made ugly and wrong so

14

that it fails to bring vivid satisfactions, we may grow to feel unworthy and cringing. We may become afraid of ourselves and of our own impulses as well as of temptation. And, in addition, we may feel irritable and upset.

When we are unable to gain a sense of achievement in life, as when we feel incapable of carrying out tasks that lie before us, we also are bothered. Anyone who has tried a job that's too hard for him knows this only too well. Whenever a person is expected to do things which he is actually not able to do, he feels lost. He feels overpowered and small and help-less. Panicky, perhaps, and embittered. "I'm incapable. So what's the use?"

Similarly, if the recognition we crave is denied us, resent-ment mounts. A person may say, "I don't care anyway. So-and-so's praise isn't worth having." But, underneath, he still mutters, "I'd like to do something to get even. . . ."

Children are no different; only more helpless. Basically their reactions are the same. Emotional hunger and the starva-tion from satisfactions which are denied them, bring *hurt* and *fear* and *resentment* in wake.

"But," we may protest, "these things are too complex. How can a child know?"

Children are acutely aware of our feelings toward them. It's hard to fool them. They know, for instance, when they're loved or not loved. Take Ricky, a seven-year-old who was brought to the psychologist's office. His parents and teachers had tried every sort of discipline to make him get over his lack of concentration and his "laziness" in school. "We've punished and rewarded and spanked and cajoled. But nothing does any good."

Ricky himself stated his case clearly. "My mom," he said, "she stays busy all day long over *me*. She cooks special cereal for me, the kind that's extra good for children. Only I can't stand it. She knits swell sweaters for me; but just between you and me, I'd rather have the store kind like all the other kids.

15

If you ask me, I think the trouble is she doesn't care too much for boys. She doesn't love a lot. She just goes buzzing around, mad most of the time."

Somewhat later, when Ricky was telling about himself, he connected his school problem with his mother's lack of loving. "In school, you see, I keep so busy wishing she'd really love me, I haven't any time left over for work. Then I get scared of what's going to happen and I try to work. But I never get anything finished. I just sit and draw ugly faces sticking their tongues out. Only I have to erase them fast so I won't get punished and then they don't do me any good!"

Ricky's emotional hunger lay at the bottom of his problem. Ricky wasn't a bad child. He was a hurt child. He was hungry for love. His laziness and his lack of concentration were his ways of showing that hurt and fear lay on his mind. His ugly drawings were his way of saying, "My mother doesn't understand me. She makes me mad."

It is easy to see that further starving would do Ricky no good. On the contrary, supplying him with the nourishment he needed—this was obviously the soundest measure to take.

Antonia, eleven, was the youngest in a family of musically gifted children. Musical accomplishment was the one and only sort of achievement which the whole family valued and appreciated. But Antonia wasn't musical and her life was one long tantrum. She yelled and stormed at her mother and father. She kicked and fought with her brothers and sisters. "I can't, I can't," shrieked Antonia. And then, with resentment apparent, she told her story.

"They keep scolding me and nagging. 'Don't you have ears, Antonia? Can't you hear? That's the wrong note you're striking. Go out of the room till you can come back and play properly. You're so stubborn, Antonia, you drive us insane.'"

When Antonia was tested for her musical ability, she was found to be actually incapable of discerning the wrong notes. She was tone-deaf. "I try so hard, I get all tight inside. I'm

16

afraid of what will happen. Then I don't want to try any more. And I catch myself whispering, 'I'd like to shove everybody in the whole wide world down the back stairs and slam the door.'"

Through no fault of her own, Antonia could not achieve what was expected of her. She was physically incapable of it. By making it the one and only important accomplishment in life, her family was robbing her of the chance for securing not only achievement but also their recognition, appreciation and love. Lacking the emotional nourishment that she needed, Antonia felt hurt and fearful and resentful to boot.

But when she showed how she felt, things only grew worse. She was made unacceptable and bad.

"They don't think I'm worth anything. I can't do anything right. I'm so different, I often think I'm a stepchild and don't really belong." And then, with a long wail, the last of the indignities came out. *"They don't understand me. They don't know how I feel."*

There was no one in the whole wide world who understood her and accepted her feelings. And this made every other hurtful thing worse.

THE WATCHWORD IS "WATCHING"

As with Ricky, starving Antonia further would only have increased her difficulties. Supplying her with what she needed was the only sound direction to take.

When a child feels a lack of love, a lack of belonging, when he feels that his yearning for bodily pleasure is wrong, when he feels that he is incapable of achieving what people expect and want of him, and—most of all—when he feels unaccepted —then the world is indeed very black.

He struggles to get out of the abyss. But he is so dismayed and bewildered that he can only stumble and slip.

If we are to lead him from the darkness, we must first of all watch him quietly and patiently and with every ounce of

17

tenderness we can muster. The more fully we understand and accept a child's feelings, the better will our guidance be.

No one accepted Antonia when she said, "I can't." No one noticed that she was hurt and fearful and angry. No one took time out to see and hear and understand how she felt. They didn't with Ricky either. If they had, they would have known far better what to do.

For one thing, they would have seen the importance of supplying these children with the emotional nourishment for which they were starving. Possibly more love of itself would have made Ricky's problem vanish. Finding things Antonia was capable of doing and giving her recognition for them would have helped her problems disappear. The feeding of emotional wants would have eased some of the pain so that subsequent discipline would not have been counteracted continuously by fresh spurts of hurt and anger and fear.

When a child's behavior makes discipline necessary, we can be sure that he is saying in some roundabout fashion, "I'm hurt!" "I'm afraid!" or "I'm angry . . . I feel resentful and nasty and mean!" That many things contribute to such feelings, we shall discover as we go on.

Suffice it to say now, one thing is certain: The more carefully we watch, the more keenly we hear, the more truly will we become attuned to what the child is actually feeling.

Here, then, are the beginning steps in learning to discipline so that a child grows in stature and strength and wholeness:

LISTEN so as to hear!
WATCH so as to see!
Try to UNDERSTAND WHAT YOUR CHILD IS FEELING
so thoroughly that you can
PUT IT INTO WORDS!

Then you'll be ready to take the next step in learning to discipline wisely and well.

18

3. Show him you know how he feels

Suppose the person nearest and dearest to you doesn't love you as much as you want? What do you do? Suffer in silence? Take it quietly? Learn to like it? . . . Would you make further deprivation a recipe for cure? Or would you say in downright fashion, "I know I don't get enough loving. In some way I've got to make that old pill of mine give me more."

When you feel misunderstood, what do you do? Do you tell yourself that going without understanding is good for you? That you're better off without it? Or do you rustle about trying, in one way or another, to find the understanding you crave?

When a person feels deprived, he normally attempts to find what he lacks. He may not try wisely, but he tries nonetheless.

"When I feel that John isn't giving me enough affection," one young wife admitted, "I get weepy, I'm so hurt. I go sniffling around hoping he'll notice and be sorry and love me more."

"I get the shakes and jitters," confessed another. "I get scared stiff that Tom's tired of me, and then I get mad and figure that if I yell enough I'll make him come 'round."

We may tell ourselves, "Look, we're getting nowhere this

19

way. It's silly to be hurt. It's nonsense to be fearful. It's ugly to be mad. So stop it. Act sensibly." But somehow we can't stop. The hurt and fear and anger seem to spring up from nowhere. They rise at unexpected moments. "I thought I had them under control. And then, bam, out they come."

In contrast, if we manage to correct the ill and secure a good, full measure of emotional nourishment, we feel much better. The ugly emotions are not so apt to appear.

It's the same with a child. The more normal he is, the more he'll keep after us for the nourishment he really needs. The less he gets of it, the more hurt and fearful and resentful he'll grow. The more he secures, the more he'll become the kind of person who is happy and healthy and sound.

"You mean if he shouts for a lollipop, give it to him no matter what?"

But that's not it! We're not speaking of supplying his every whim. We're speaking of the big, important things, necessities like milk or vegetables. If a child cries for a toy in a store window, we don't need to think we're depriving him in any deep and hurtful way by refusing it. But if he cries for more affection, that's a very different matter.

And yet, when a child is very obviously seeking a certain kind of really basic satisfaction, we may still feel that granting it will spoil him too much.

Ronnie's mother did just this. "He tags after me like a little puppy dog. He clings to me like a kitten. I can't leave the room without his mooing like a calf. Now I ask you! He's not a child; he's a menagerie!

"I haven't time to fuss over him in the mornings; I've got the big house to go over. I haven't time to fuss over him in the afternoons; I've got dinner to get for five people. I haven't time to fuss over him in the evenings; after all, the older children and my husband are around then and they keep me in a whirl. And anyway, I don't want to run my life around Ronnie. I don't want to pamper him that much. So I say, as calmly

20

as I can, 'Go 'way and play.' I've talked sweetly and I've yelled till my throat's gotten tired. I've scolded and bribed. I've tried every type of cure to keep him out from under my feet. But all he does is get worse."

"He wants his mommie to love him like you do me!"

Had Ronnie's mother tried harder to feel how Ronnie felt, she would have seen clearly and heard clearly that Ronnie was seeking more love. If he had been lacking in physical nourishment, she would have thought it her duty to make it up to him. She would certainly not have said, "I'll spoil him if I satisfy his hunger." But because his was an emotional instead of a physical hunger, she did just this.

Unfortunately, many of us have followed in similar pathways. We never learned anything else.

But now we want to do a better job. So we'll need, above all, to reorient ourselves on this matter of satisfying emotional hunger.

✦ In the first place, we'll study our child to see how he shows us that he needs more love, more chances for achievement, more recognition, more appreciation or understanding, more of this or of that emotional food. In the second place, we'll do our utmost to supply whatever he needs. After that, we'll watch closely what happens. We'll probably see his face growing happier and his bearing more sturdy and sure.

But even then some disciplinary problems will most likely remain. Nine chances out of ten, at least a *part of the hurt and fear and anger will still run on.*

This may seem to stand for failure. Actually it doesn't. There are perfectly good reasons for the persistence of some of the troublesome signs even after we've done all we can to satisfy a child's needs.

To understand how this works, let's turn our focus onto our own feelings. Let's think, for instance, what happens when a best beloved gives us too little affection. Aren't hurt and fear and anger the usual results? Then if more affection comes back our way the hurt and fear and anger are apt to let down. But they don't vanish completely—just like that! "Tom's been sweet to me again. But I still get mad at him for no good reason. I can't seem to forget what he's done in the past."

Children can't always forget either. Many times, after the hurtful thing has long since vanished, the hurt and fear and anger run on.

Says Betsy's father, "When Betsy was two years old, she used to get so silly at the dinner table that I'd stick her out on the back porch. She'd howl bloody murder. But invariably when I went to get her, she'd turn and slap at me. That was before I knew better. I'd failed to see, then, that Betsy had been acting silly because she felt like such an outsider. For one reason, her mother and grandmother and I had left her out by talking so perpetually over her head that she'd gotten a sense of not belonging in the group. Then I made her feel

22

even more lack of belonging by shoving her off by herself and isolating her on the back porch. Believe you me, I stopped and gave her all the belongingness I could as soon as I found this out. That was a year ago. But to this day she avoids the back porch as if it had nettles growing in it. When I take her through it her little face still darkens and she turns on me, involuntarily, and raises her hand."

Betsy hadn't forgotten. The hurt and the anger had not completely vanished. Remnants were still there even though the emotional lack had been supplied.

WHEN YOU SPOT A NEED, MEET IT ALL YOU CAN

We know now that a part of our job as parents and teachers is to help satisfy a child's deep and important emotional needs. We'll discover more about how to do this. But as we read on, let's remember that we can't expect perfection either of a child or of ourselves.

It is almost impossible for parents to meet a child's emotional needs completely. Sometimes complexities enter. For one thing, an emotional want may lie hidden like hidden hunger. A child, to all intents and purposes, may have every need satisfied. And yet he may still be starving, although from the surface this is impossible to see.

For another thing, external pressures often enter which parents cannot prevent. Economic stress, illness, overcrowded homes, lacks in privacy, and numerous other unfortunate elements are beyond the parents' control.

For still another thing, the parents' own wants and needs may be at war with a child's, and the parents may not even recognize that this is so.

As one mother put it, "I never realized before, but now I'm beginning to see that all the little things my nine-year-old did that bothered me were really hitting a responsive chord in my own make-up. I was always the one to miss words in spelling. I was always the one not to read a book right. I pushed and tried but I didn't get better. So, when he didn't spell or read exactly right either, I pushed him. That only made him worse, but I couldn't seem to help it! Until I realized I was reacting to him just as if he were me!"

Her own unsatisfied needs had blinded her. Because she had felt too little sense of achievement in her own childhood, she had pushed herself beyond her capacity. Now inad-

"Nobody around here understands how a fellow feels. I'll make them sorry."

vertently she was wishing her own needs onto her youngster. She wanted him to achieve beyond his capacity to make up for her lack.

Most of us fail our children in one respect or another. We do this unwittingly. And yet as we do it, hurt and anger and fear are apt to arise.

We shouldn't blame ourselves. It's no use sitting down to weep and berate ourselves. A far better and more constructive way is to ask, "What can we do *now?*"

So far we can see these things:

> If a child MISBEHAVES,
> we'll recognize that he must have
> UNSATISFIED EMOTIONAL NEEDS
> or that he is still expressing
> HURT, FEAR or ANGER
> for LACKS IN THE PAST.
> If we find that a child has an
> unsatisfied emotional need,
> we'll try to SATISFY it
> all we can.

> We won't be surprised, though, if
> REMNANTS of the HURT or FEAR or ANGER
> still hang on.

> We must also help a child
> RELEASE and LESSEN these.

As we repeat the above principles, we probably will stumble and hesitate over the last. "How shall we go about trying to lessen the hurt and the fear and the anger? How shall we start?"

FEEL HOW HE FEELS AND SAY IT TO HIM

In parody of a famous couplet, every parent might pray,

> Oh wad some power the giftie gie
> To know my child and feel as he.

The ability to feel as he feels can be a great source of strength. It can carry a child and parent beyond the small struggles for supremacy, beyond the querulous argument, beyond the cudgel and whip into activities that supply needs and heal hurt and fear and anger.

Ronnie's mother came to understand the importance of feeling *with* a child instead of against him. The scene changed

25

then from what it had been. Now when Ronnie put on the mama-baby business, his mother no longer came back with a stream of talk. She no longer scolded or punished or persuaded or bribed. She did not call over her shoulder without even turning, "Run on. Go play. Stop following mother around."

Instead, she tried a new set of procedures in accordance with the new ways of disciplining a child. She stood still and watched Ronnie and saw the hungry look in his face. She listened and heard his whimper and the sound of his small, stumbling feet. And she said to herself, *"I must understand so thoroughly what he is feeling that I can put it into words."*

So she asked herself, *"What is he feeling?"* And the answer came swiftly, "He wants to stay with me. He doesn't want me to leave him. He wants more loving. He wants to be close."

Then she asked herself a second question, *"How can I say his feeling back to him?* How can I put it so as to communicate to him that I know how he feels?

"Why, put it straight, of course, only simply. Make what I say a kind of reflection of what he feels, as if I were mirroring it in my speech. THINK WHAT HE IS FEELING AND SAY IT ALOUD."

Next time Ronnie's feet came tapping after her, she turned toward him and said, "Ronnie's feet are saying, 'Tap, tap, mommie. I want to come with you.'"

Next time Ronnie clutched at her skirt, she looked down and said, "Ronnie wants to hang onto mommie."

Next time Ronnie screamed for her to stay in his room at bedtime, she answered, "You don't want me to go away."

She kept saying his feelings back to him consistently. "You want me to stay with you all the time, honey." . . . "You don't like to have mommie do anything but stay with you." . . . "It makes you lonely when mommie turns out the light and leaves."

As she did this, she noticed that she herself began to feel

26

differently. Instead of remaining perpetually conscious of her own grievances, she found herself growing increasingly conscious of Ronnie and *his* grievances. And she felt a welling up of sympathy and love.

At first none of the new ways seemed to make any impression. Ronnie still clung; he still yammered. But gradually Ronnie's mother became aware of a new thing happening.

Ronnie was nodding soberly each time she mirrored his feelings and in a subdued small whisper he was repeating, "Ronnie wants his mommie. Ronnie doesn't want his mommie to go 'way."

Came a day when his voice was no longer small and subdued. It rose in downright and loud declaration. "Ronnie wants mommie *all* the time."

And then, suddenly, Ronnie smiled. He grinned up at his mother and announced squarely, "Mommie knows now . . . Now Ronnie go play."

Without another glance in her direction, he turned and trudged out to the yard and his sandbox, secure in his mind that his mother did know and understand.

She had gotten his feelings so thoroughly into her mind and heart that she had been able to put them into words for him. But that was not all she had done. In seeing and hearing and feeling *with* him, her attitude had changed. She was no longer blaming and condemning him. She was no longer thinking he was just a big nuisance. She had *understood* him at last. She had *accepted* his feelings and had acknowledged their reality. She had taken him as he was instead of prodding him into being what she wanted him to be without consideration of either his needs or his hurts.

With Ronnie, as with other children, such handling has proved effective. It is far more healing than the irritation of argument. To small Ronnie it brought knowledge that he was *worth* being seen and listened to. It carried to him a firm conviction that he was accepted and understood. He no longer needed to clamor for greater closeness. His mother and he were together. He was no longer alone.

Far more often than we imagine, *understanding acceptance* and the *mirroring of feelings* are all that are needed to bring positive results. This holds for children of all ages and for grownups as well.

At first this may sound silly, but as we think more about it the idea isn't so absurd. A person always does better when he approaches a thing with good will rather than with brooding resentment or anger. And obviously, good will comes more readily when a person feels that he is accepted and understood.

Suppose you yourself have spent a sleepless night and are now rushing to get breakfast. The baby cries. The telephone rings. Before you know it, the toast has burned.

Your nerves give way and you let out a long string of invective. You're mad and discouraged. At this particular moment fixing another batch of toast is just too much! And yet you know it must be done.

Suppose then that hubby yells at you from the bathroom where he is shaving. Suppose he scolds and berates you for your clumsiness. How do you react? You certainly don't go about fixing the toast with any verve or good will.

But suppose his voice comes acceptantly. "That's a darn shame, darling. It makes you furious, I know!" You feel he's *with* you; not *against* you. He gives you this feeling not only by what he says but by the way he says it. You know he knows how you feel and this brings you comfort.

Suddenly things aren't so black and you call back, relieved, "Thanks, darling. I'll have a new batch of toast done in a moment. It's only a little thing."

Understanding acceptance and the mirroring of your feelings were all that were needed to make you *want* to cooperate.

Every one of us has known the bleakness of not having our real feelings understood. Every one of us has known the immense relief that comes when some one person has paused and listened and has finally comprehended. There was suddenly something good in the world—a relationship that augmented our own worth. We were suddenly better able to communicate. We felt sudden new strength and a kind of wholeness. We were better people for that day and the next.

The ear that hears and does not merely listen, the eye that sees and does not merely look, and, above all, the earnest desire to feel *with* a child so that we are able to say his feelings aloud for him—these measures are immensely helpful. Many times they can of themselves replace the old ways of disciplining. At other times, further measures are needed. Let's look at these next.

4. Getting the "badness" out

I BEGAT A BRAT

"Why is my child so naughty? He fights with everything in sight from his father and me to the dog."

"Mine's an angel at home. But not at school! Yesterday his teacher was leaning over the desk across from his and he rapped her on the rear end with his ruler and told her to take her fanny out of his way."

"Mine's so destructive, there's nothing left whole in the house."

"Mine's sulky and disagreeable. When company comes he won't open his mouth except to pull out his bubble gum into long sticky streamers."

"My daughter doesn't ever look where she's going. If I've told her once, I've told her a hundred times. She's so careless she broke her toe, burned her hand and knocked a tooth out all in one month. Just because she can't bother to stop and look."

"Why does my child always fuss over going to bed? It's screech! Screech! Mo-other, I wannanother glass of water! . . . Screech! Screech! I gotta go! . . . Screech! I gotta go again! . . . Screech, screech! There's a bug crawling over my face! . . . There's a burglar trying to get in the window! . . . Hey Mo-o-ther, do-o-n't close the door!"

"Why on earth does my child suck his thumb till it looks like a washboard with warts?"

All these trying types of behavior are signs that children are hurt, afraid, angry; perhaps all three. Either in their past lives or in the present, some of their basic emotional needs have not been adequately met.

Father: "Don't you dare talk to your mother like that."
Daughter: "So you *don't* want to know what I think."

"But," you say, "we've checked and we can't see where anything is wrong. At least not now. There used to be before we knew better. We've corrected all that, though. And he still acts like a brat!"

Perhaps, then, *he is carrying over some of his feelings from the past into the present.* Perhaps, by his tumultuous behavior, he is bringing out some grudge that was born in the past.

"But," you counter once more, "he isn't hurt or fearful or

31

angry. He never was. He never had any reason to be. We've looked over the whole picture and we can't see a thing that could possibly have hurt him or made him angry or afraid."

For various and sundry reasons, we may try our best to see the whole picture and yet we may not see quite the whole. For one thing, *we can't see into our child's unconscious mind.* We can't see the hurt or fear or anger that has lodged there. We can't recognize that some of the things he is doing are expressions of *unconscious* feelings. Nor can we identify these unconscious feelings. For they are not coming out as they really are. They are coming out in strange disguises and shapes.

No matter how old we are, we all bring out unconscious feelings in strange forms and guises. This comes about in a complex fashion which, put as simply as possible, runs something like this.

In the beginning, a hurt of some sort always starts the chain of events. The hurt, in turn, has always resulted from that old specter, starvation; a lack of nourishment for some basic need.

As illustration, let's take a child whose basic need for achievement has not been adequately fed.

In the beginning, young Tom, red and husky, raises his voice in a loud infant wail to tell his parents he's hungry. This, for him, is an achievement. It's his only way of communicating a want and securing surcease from it. "But," says Tom's mother, "it's not time for him to be fed yet."

"No, it's not," his father agrees. "For Pete's sake let's not spoil him."

They believe it's important to keep a child on a regular schedule. They've been told this over and over again. And so they close their ears and fail to hear what he says.

Obviously, they are doing what they think is best for him. But it has at least one unfortunate result. Tommy has failed in his very first attempt to set matters right in life and to ease his pain. The hunger pangs in his middle are left to run on until his parents bring the bottle according to the clock. The assuaging of hunger, then, is *their* achievement, not his. What *he* did was wrong.

Young Tommy grows. He grows to the point where mother tries to train him to use the pot. It seems he never will learn until, when he is quite a sizable boy, already walking, he finally manages. For him this is a great victory, an achievement at last. So he reaches in with both hands and picks up what's in the pot and carries it proudly to his mother.

"Tommy!" she shrieks. "You dirty boy. Put that down. Dirty! Icky! Don't you *ever* do that again!"

Suddenly, his achievement is no longer worth anything. What *he* did was wrong.

Comes a day, a year or more later, when Tommy discovers the way to turn on the garden hose. The handle, he finds, goes 'round and 'round in a most fascinating manner. And zzishsh! A stream of water spurts across the lawn. To Tommy this is a wonderful thing. A great achievement! He is master of the universe! He has accomplished a gigantic feat. Tommy has discovered remote control.

But look! Here comes daddy rushing down the path. "Tommy!" he yells. "If you don't cut out the mischief, I'll smack you so hard you won't forget!" In an instant, Tommy's newest achievement has been brought to naught. Again what *he* did was wrong.

Still a year or so later, "Look, Daddy, I made an airplane!"

"No, Tommy. That's not the way to do it. The propeller's not right. Bring it here, I'll fix it."

Or, "Mommie, look, I drew a camel."

"Fine!" absent-mindedly, "only a camel has *two* humps, like this." And mother takes over with firm, swift strokes.

This sort of thing happens on and on. Nothing Tommy does is ever quite as it should be. Nothing is quite good enough. He's never right; he's always wrong. His need for achievement is blocked here and there and everywhere all along. He doesn't feel capable.

This is the hurt!

But it isn't the individual episode that has hurt him. It's the big pile of small episodes that have stacked up.

In his mind Tommy says, "I-want-to-achieve BUT they-never-let-me."

And then, fast, another thought comes. "If they weren't around to pick on me, I would be doing all right. They're horrid! They're old meanies. I hate them. I wish they were dead!"

This is the anger!

And then, faster still, "I mustn't say or think such things. If I do, something terrible might happen. If they found out, they might not want me any more. Then where would I be?" Or, "If they found out, they'd punish me dreadfully!" Or, "If I stay mad I might do something really too awful!"

All of this is the fear!

The anger and the fear have gotten jumbled together. The resentment by now has created so much anxiety and tension that Tommy tries his utmost to cover it up. "I mustn't be bad-mad. I'm really *not* that way. I'm not mad at them. I don't hate them. I never said that I did! Why should I? They're so wonderful to me; they *never* hurt me. I love them so much I don't mind what they do. There now! I don't have to be afraid any more!"

Then he runs and throws his arms around them in extra big hugs to reassure himself that he does love them dearly, that they haven't hurt him, that his anger never existed and that he has no cause for fear. He denies the hurt and fear and anger and pushes the whole conglomeration from his conscious mind into his unconscious. He dumps them there and puts the lid on tight. He forgets that he's ever been hurt or fearful or angry. It's as if he were saying, "Now those dreadful feelings don't bother me any more!" But he's wrong. They do.

34

They're hidden but they're not gone. They stir and press in his unconscious mind. They boil and bubble. They try to get out.

Then several different things may happen.

For one, he manages to keep the troublesome feelings under cover. But as he does this, he has to hold the lid down constantly on all feelings. As a result, the fine impulses in the unconscious can not come out either. A person's creative drive, a person's urge to love, a person's strength to fight the fair fight must also be held under. He can't let any feelings come out spontaneously or vigorously for fear that the forbidden ones will sneak out with them. He becomes withdrawn and shy, ill at ease, afraid of his own shadow and often of everything else. Or he becomes the "Little Angel," "mama's darling"; the extra GOOD child who never does wrong. Very seldom do we realize that TOO GOOD is a DISGUISE for being TOO BAD.

Another possibility is that the pressure of the unwelcome feelings becomes too great and springs a leak, in the same way that boiling water may spring a leak in a kettle if the steam it generates has no proper channel for release.

Meanwhile, our child is still trying to hide the unwanted feelings from sight. If they were to leak out in their original form, he would recognize them. But this he must not do. So he finds a device for letting them reappear in such a way that he won't recognize them. He *masks* them. He *lets them out in disguises only* and he keeps them disguised in two ways. By changing their form. And by changing their target.

Our Tommy, as example, does not say to his father or mother, "I hate you, I'd like to kill you dead." Instead, he has temper tantrums to slay them. (Here he is changing the form.) At times he is stubborn and negative and disguises his resentment in refusals to wash and dress and eat. (He is still changing the form.) At other times he masks by letting out aggression on his teacher, on the dog or on his friends. (This

35

is changing the target.) For if the thing or person against whom he directs his anger is other than his parents, he disguises the fact that he is angry at them. To Tommy, sticking a pin into the dog is a far cry from sticking a pin into his father. And so it may serve as a successful mask.

A child may also let out in other ways the emotion he doesn't dare or want to see. He may let it out against vague opponents by stealing cars from unknown people. He may let it out in lying and unsocial behavior against anyone who comes along. Or, more curiously still, he may turn it against himself. This he does, for instance, by getting sick. He may develop a skin eruption that lets the "dirtiness" out all over him. He may get a "pain in the neck" or eyes that water and "weep." He may have continuous accidents or make himself miserable and unhappy for no good reason except the real one underneath—to use himself as a target on which the unwanted feelings can be aimed.

No matter which of these disguises a person uses, the result in the long run is much the same. The troubled feelings are like weeds that overrun a garden and destroy the growth of blossoming things. In the unconscious great potentialities for good lie rooted. As the fear and guilt and anxiety reduce, as hampering emotions are released and dwindle, then the strengths within can flourish and produce.

With Florence, the strengths were choked under the many disguises she'd had to use in the course of her life. She was an only child. From the moment she was born, her mother devoted herself assiduously to her. Florence had to be perfect. Everything had to be well regulated and right. Her mother paid so much attention to the schedule that she had meager time left for understanding and love.

Florence started rebelling in a normal, little-child fashion. She screamed and sobbed; she kicked and hit. She grew increasingly negative, feeling in her small soul that she was not going to be prodded into becoming an automaton who would have to give up her own sense of achievement in answering to her mother's every demand. She felt, somehow, that she had a right to be herself.

Her mother wanted her to eat; well, she wouldn't. Her mother wanted her to keep her bed and her pants dry; well, she wouldn't. She hated and resented her mother at times, although she did not acknowledge this in so many words. The more her mother punished, the worse Florence got.

A defeated look crept into her mother's face and Florence saw this. It made her feel that she was making her mother suffer too greatly. In combination with the ever-increasing punishments, it also made Florence feel that she was too terribly bad. How could her mother endure her? Gradually she shoved into her unconscious mind the resentment she felt.

She could not let it come out directly in hate for her mother. She was too afraid. And so, as she grew, Florence became a very good child. Her mother drew a breath of relief and patted herself on the back for having disciplined her daughter successfully. "It wasn't in vain."

But, down underneath, in the child's unconscious, the hurt and anxiety and resentment were present still and continued to motivate Florence. They made her anxious and fearful. They pressed so painfully that she had to let them out. But, at the same time, she had to disguise them. For one thing, she could not admit into consciousness any hatred for her mother, so she disguised this by turning it into hate for herself. "I'm no good. I'm worthless." She knew before she tried anything that she wouldn't be able to do it. She kept repeating, "I can't."

In high school, the principal looked across the desk at her. "Florence, you've got a brilliant mind but you're not using it." Florence glanced up in astonishment. All the intelligence tests in the world couldn't prove to her that she was brilliant. Way down inside she knew she was no good.

By belittling herself, by shearing herself of self-confidence, by filling herself with inferiority feelings, Florence kept pitting against herself the resentment that had originally generated toward her mother. She had used her own self as a substitute target so that the badness would not show.

Many substitute targets are used in today's world. Childhood resentment that has piled up for years may, for instance, come out against society in juvenile delinquency or adult crime. It may come out disguised in prejudice against minority groups, in religious intolerance, in race riots and war. It may come out in fights with companions and co-workers, or in the bitter word against one's boss, one's wife, one's child. As long as it is not directed against the original target, it stays hidden or comes out disguised, regardless of the harm. This fact must lead every thoughtful person into contemplation of an inexplicable phenomenon. Here we stand, many adults in our culture, convinced that we must crush childhood aggression which spreads its hands and kicks and screams in comparative ineffectuality. We must force it under and hold its head down, no matter what sort of monstrosity evolves later when it finally catches its breath.

It is a strange thing that feelings which we do not even know are inside us can not only exist but can actually motivate what we do.

The result is obviously devastating and destructive. For, being blind to a thing, we can in no way handle it. Like an infection whose identity and origin we do not know, it runs on and on, attacking where it may, completely outside our knowledge and control.

LET THE POISON OUT

When pus accumulates and forms an abscess, the abscess must be opened and drained. If this isn't done the infection spreads. In the end, it may destroy the individual. Just so with feelings. The "badness" must come out. The hurts and

38

fears and anger must be released and drained. Otherwise, these too may destroy the individual.

Let's see what happens to seven-year-old Martin. He runs across the gravel path and skids. His feet fly out from under him and down he goes. A red, streaky blotch appears across one knee.

"It hurts! It hurts!" he screams.

Mother: "Don't cry. It doesn't hurt, dear!"
Junior, angrily: "Who told you it doesn't?"

"Hey there," shouts his mother. "Cut it out, Martin. Pick yourself up and act like a man. It's nothing but a scratch. It doesn't hurt."

Martin looks daggers but he stops crying and goes on his way. That night, though, when his mother leans over his bed, she finds him whimpering in his sleep.

Martin is no different from many children. We've heard

plenty of this sort of thing. "Don't cry! Don't be a sissy! It doesn't hurt." In other words, "Don't let the hurt out. Hold it under. Don't let it show."

But as children hold in the hurt it only grows. And other hurts join it. The hurt of being misunderstood is not least among these.

On the other hand, as a child gets the hurt off his chest to a person who listens and accepts his feeling, the hurt seems somehow less important.

Suppose you bang your finger with a hammer, what do you do? Say it doesn't hurt? Or cuss a bit? Why? Because it makes the hurt seem less intense. Or suppose your feelings are hurt. Aren't you relieved if you can spill about them to someone who appreciates how you feel?

Don's father knew this, in contrast to Martin's. So, he stopped and looked and listened and showed Don he knew how he felt. "It sure hurts, son!" he mirrored Don's feelings. And then he did something else.

"Tell me about it!" he said.

"I was running," Don sobbed, "and those darn fool pebbles they tripped me and made me skid. It sure hurts, it does."

"Want to show me?"

"Oh gee, Pop, it's bloody. The blood's going all over. It hurts like the dickens . . . Why did I have to go and do it? It's a mess . . ."

"It feels pretty miserable."

"It sure does, Pop!" And then, suddenly, without any apparent reason for the shift, "It's not so bad now. I gotta get going or I'll miss the other kids. So long, Pop."

Although it may not be too apparent, there had been a natural reason for the shift. Don had released and drained enough of the hurt for him to move on more happily.

Don's father, in turn, had done several things: He had *observed sensitively* and had seen how his child felt. He had *reflected his child's feelings*. He had given Don a chance to

40

talk out, to *release* and drain the hurt. He hadn't argued or scolded. He had *accepted* what came.

As a result, Don had gotten over his hurt far more readily than Martin. And what was even more important, no nasty remnants had been pushed inside.

Another thing that is important for adults to know is that children often use their muscles in place of their mouths. They act out their troubles with hands and arms and bodies. They release the poison through what they do as well as through what they say.

Children often PLAY OUT their
feelings instead of TALKING OUT
how they feel.

Three-year-old Sally did this spontaneously with her fear of dogs. She'd been bitten one day and thereafter yelled bloody murder whenever the most innocuous puppy hove into view.

Her parents had tried bribing and petting. "If only Sally wouldn't scream." In final exasperation they ridiculed her. "You silly crybaby!" Her screams only grew worse. But one morning her mother noticed that Sally did a curious thing.

She was playing with her crayons. She scribbled a big brown splotch onto the paper and then began talking to it as though it were something alive. Her mother watched and listened and tried to get what Sally was feeling so that she might mirror it if this seemed wise.

"Bad doggie!" Sally was saying. "I don't like you. Bad, bad dog. You bite."

Much to her mother's surprise Sally stamped on the paper and pummeled it with her feet "like a small dancing dervish." Then, with an angelic smile, Sally announced, "He's dead now. Bad dog's all gone."

"This is something!" thought Sally's mother. "This is like that new stuff about discipline I recently read. What's my next step now? Oh yes. I must reflect Sally's feelings. Easily. Not intrusively. As if I were playing the game with her and echoing her thoughts."

Aloud her mother said, "You don't like that mean old dog. You want him to be dead and gone."

"Uh-huh." Sally nodded and requested, "You make a bad doggie now."

Her mother drew a dog roughly on another piece of paper. "Here's another dog for Sally. *Tell me* or *show me about this one.*"

"He's bad too. He bites Sally. You're naughty, you bad, bad dog." And again Sally stamped and jumped up and down on the dog's picture with all her might.

For days this game went on. But finally, Sally's theme song changed. Suddenly she announced, "I like *this* doggie. He's good. He's not bitey. He's a crybaby dog."

A few days later out on the sidewalk, when Sally spied the neighbors' old black spaniel she no longer screamed as she had at his approach for weeks. She stood quite still and waited till he waddled up to her, sniffling. Then she put out her hand and touched his back.

"Poor little doggie," she soothed him. "Don't you be a crybaby. Sally's not a crybaby any more."

As we've seen earlier, hurt and fear produce anger. With Sally the release of all three had brought about new and happier feelings. It had made Sally stronger, more courageous, more whole.

Almost always this occurs. *When enough of the negative feelings have drained off and have been accepted, then more positive feelings come in.*

Even when parents realize the truth of this statement, it still is exceedingly difficult to permit the release of feeling when anger is uppermost in a child's mind. For anger and resentment in our culture are considered ignoble and undesirable. They are emotions which we commonly believe must

42

be kept down. They are feelings over which a person should feel guilty and ashamed—especially if they are directed against a father or mother. Then they are not only undesirable, they are utterly unspeakable. And yet they exist at times in almost every child.

"I hate you, you witch!" splutters twelve-year-old Jenifer. "You're the meanest woman I ever saw."

Nothing daunted, Jenifer's mother mirrored Jenifer's feelings. Without anger. Without condemnation. Without feeling inside herself that Jenifer needed to be taken down a peg for her lack of respect. But with loving conviction, "Since Jenifer feels this way, she'd better get the badness out."

Aloud Jenifer's mother reflected, "You hate me worse than you can say."

"You bet I do."

"Perhaps you can tell me more about it. I really want to hear."

"You'll only punish me if I tell you."

"You think I'll punish you like I used to. But I was mistaken. I've learned a lot lately. I know now that mean feelings are better out than in, and that it's best for all of us if you can get them off your chest."

Jenifer looked at her mother, astonishment clear in her face. "Okay, then, here goes. You weren't fair. You never are. You keep nagging at me. You keep making me do things. I'm *never* going to set the table again or make the beds! I'm not going to take out the garbage. I've been nothing more than a slave and it's got to stop."

"You feel as if we've made you do too much."

"Oh skip it. I don't know."

But the same evening, in came Jenifer, gay as a lark. "Here, Mud, let me set the table. I picked some roses to put in the center so maybe I'll use the yellow cloth."

Take Heinie, six, who has been on a hunger strike in spite of parental implorings galore.

Today father approaches with the new look in his eye. Inside he is thinking, "Yes, I know how you feel, kid, and I'm prepared to really take it with understanding. When you tell or show me, I'm not going to scold or argue you out of it. I'm going to *accept*." To Heinie he says very simply, "You don't want to eat," reflecting what Heinie has shown.

"It's stinkin' food. I hate it. I'll throw it under the table."

"You want to throw it." Father nods.

" 'Cause I won't eat it," defiantly from Heinie.

"You just don't want to," from father. His tone holds neither the sting of sarcasm nor the patience of martyrdom. He speaks with sincere kindness and his air is one of waiting, which at this moment is far better than any invitation to tell or show more.

"It's nasty. It smells. I can't stand it. I'll throw it down the drainpipe. I'll throw mom down too. I'll drown her. And you, too. You all smell, you do."

"You feel mean-mad at us."

"I'll throw all this stuff in your face."

"I know you'd like to, you feel so mean . . ."

Heinie nods and then, truculent still, eats a few spoonfuls. Gradually day by day, as he keeps on bringing out more and more of the "badness," the "goodness" increases. He eats more and eats more cheerfully, and the tirades give way to fun and laughter and a friendly recounting of recent events.

Many times this is the way it happens. When enough of the hurt and fear and anger have been released, they diminish. They stop pushing from within. They stop springing out in compulsive ways, disguising what lies underneath so that it can not be dealt with. After enough of the "badness" has come out, the "goodness" appears.

Sometimes when a parent starts with this new approach, a child is distrustful. His father and mother have always been unacceptant of his negative feelings. He cannot believe that they are now making an about-face. Then, as Jenifer's mother

44

did, it's wise to explain that a new sort of approach is being made. "I've never let you show me before how you really felt. I've scolded you, I know. But now we're turning over a new leaf. I don't care how mean you feel, I'm hoping you'll share it with me!" Or, "I've made a mistake in not letting you tell or show me. But I know better now!"

No matter what words a parent uses to define his new tactics, the attitude and feeling behind the words are what really count. A child senses whether a parent really means what he says. A child soon sees if true acceptance is present. He senses if a parent's anger is being held in and covered with mock love and sweetness. He detects falseness and responds sincerely only to what is sincere.

As parents listen and reflect and sincerely accept a child's feelings and give the "badness" a chance to spill out—sometimes no more is needed.

For, curious as it may seem, this has been observed many times over:

When unwanted NEGATIVE FEELINGS
have been emptied out sufficiently
then—
warm and good POSITIVE FEELINGS
flow in.

When muddy water, which has dammed up, drains out from a pool, then fresh, clear water can flow in. So it is with these feelings. But the change does not happen quickly. It often takes a long time.

5. He need not run wild

"Oh," you are sighing at this point, "let's get on with discipline!" Or you are protesting, "This book is supposed to be about discipline but so far we've heard only about license. I can't let my child be unruly. I have to find some way of putting on the brakes!"

Obviously, we must have methods of stopping a child when he goes too far. We must let him see in no uncertain terms that he can't do certain things.

At this point, if we are looking for ways of curbing or limiting his actions when they grow dangerous or destructive, we are absolutely right.

Dangerous and destructive acts
must be curbed

Let's stop and think! Has anything been said about allowing dangerous or destructive acts to run on? Let's check.

Would it have been either dangerous or destructive if baby Tommy's parents had fed him when he cried and had granted him a sense that he could achieve the communication of his hunger to them? Would his mother have let a dangerous or destructive act run on if she had acknowledged his achievement of using the pot, even though he did pick up what was in it? She could so readily have preserved this sense of achievement by mirroring his feelings and saying, "Tommy

46

did it in the pot! He did, all right! And he feels good about it!"

Then she could have gone a step further. She could have suggested, "Now Tommy can put it back in the pot. That's where it goes!"

In this manner she would have done several things. She would have preserved regard for his feelings. At the same time, she would have helped Tommy to learn new ways of act-

Twins: "Mother dear, we just came in to tell you we hate you very much!"

ing. She would not have curtailed Tommy's sense of achievement. She would have *understood and accepted the feelings* and she would have *guided the actions* at one and the same time. And through it all, she would have avoided bringing on hurt or anger or fear.

HANDLING THE FEELINGS is one part of the issue. HANDLING THE ACTIONS is another part. As far as the first part goes, if we're honest we have to admit that no matter how we prod or pry, a child is going to go right on feeling the way he

47

feels. If we don't let him think his feelings aloud, he'll think them under his breath. If we make him too ashamed to think them consciously, he'll feel them in his unconscious where he is unaware of them and so can do nothing about them. But we don't stop him from feeling the feelings—no matter how weak or fearful, no matter how "bad" or "wicked" they are. They stay in him and press him into doing hurtful things even though he does not know they're there.

And so, as far as *feelings* go, the better part of wisdom is for us to accept the troubled ones, no matter how nasty they are, and to help our youngsters work them out. As for *actions*, that's another story. Here we should help a child put on the brakes.

There are limits on WHAT may be done as release.

"I know how you feel, dear, and I'm glad you're showing me. But you'll have to show me in some other way. I can't let you pull Meatball's tail."

"I can't let you slap baby brother!"

"I can't let you shoot BB shots at the kittens."

"You may not pull the curtains down, or throw ash trays at the chandelier."

"You may not put crayon marks all over the wallpaper." . . . "You may not hit daddy with that hairbrush!"

In short, a child may not do any physical HARM to any person or any object. He may not do anything that will be *harmful* or *dangerous* or *destructive*. These things are simply not allowed. These things are forbidden. They must be *stopped*.

It is especially important that children do nothing that stands to them as physical harm to their parents. They need their parents so mightily, especially when they are small, that nothing must happen to endanger a parent physically. For all the moments a child has of resentment, he also has

48

moments of love. The two are not mutually exclusive. They run together side by side—*two* currents in one stream.

"I don't want you around here," yells four-year-old Buster, kicking his mother.

At this point, his mother would best have said to Buster, "Look, dear, I can't let you kick me." She might even have held his legs to stop him or have held him off in arm's length restraint. But she didn't. She had mistaken the idea of permitting feelings with the idea of permitting actions. She had mistaken release for license, which it must not be. And so, she had let Buster kick her.

A few minutes later he burst into hysterical tears and clung, terrified, to her. "Don't go 'way, Muddy. Please, please, don't go."

He was afraid that by his own act of violence he had lost the person whom he actually loved most in the world. He was panicky at the possibility of really hurting and losing the person on whom he was most dependent for nourishment and for life.

The same sort of thing happened with five-year-old Dick. Only this time it happened when older methods of discipline were used. Dick's mother, knowing nothing about the new discipline, had reprimanded him as she did almost every hour of the day. And Dick had turned and had hit her as he had been hitting her for many months. In all this time he had not said a word out loud. Inside, though, he had muttered, "I wish you were dead, you old meanie. I'll kill you dead with this bomb!" And he had imagined that the fist with which he was hitting her was a bomb.

A short while later, Dick developed a peculiar tic. It was a sort of arm jerk, as if he were pulling his arm away from something he didn't want his hand to do, at the same time twisting his shoulder and head so as not to see. Quite unconsciously, as the psychologist explained to Dick's parents, Dick was trying to undo the imagined harm he had done his mother. By jerking his hand back he would stop it from throwing a bomb at her. By turning his head away he would manage not to see.

Many children do similar things, some in more ferocious, some in milder, fashion. But almost always, if they strike or hurt or harm a really needed or beloved person, or if they imagine they do so through destroying that person's valued property, guilt and shame are set going in their hearts. They may grow terrified of what they *think* they have done. It becomes as real to them as though they had done it in fact.

For this reason, as well as for many others, it is essential that certain *actions* be stopped. We cannot permit physical hurt or harm or destruction in any form. There are limits to WHAT a child may do by way of release.

Also—

There are limits on
WHEN and WHERE
a child acts out his feelings.

"My child always picks the worst and most embarrassing places to get out his resentments. On the street corner, waiting for a car, at the market, in the park—always in front of a million people. Always where it embarrasses me most."

That's probably one reason he does it, because he knows it will get you down and that's what he's after. Even so, you can't let it go on or you'll be so riled up yourself that you won't handle it well.

And so you'll say, "Look, Son, not here. Later on at home you can tell or show me how you feel. But not *here.*"

Not before company, that's certain. You won't be able to do a good job of acceptance with a dozen critical eyes looking on. And so, again, "Later on. Not *now.*"

Not at parties, not in crowds, not in front of neighbors. Not in these places.

50

Not while you are mixing up a cake batter or while you are talking with a sick friend over the phone. Not at these times.

The old adage "There's a time and place for everything" still holds in regard to a child's working off his feelings.

"But it's not so easy," you protest.

Indeed it isn't. Nor will we always be successful in defining WHAT and WHEN and HOW. So let's have patience with ourselves and with our child. And let's keep the weather eye searching for harmless, nondestructive ways of letting troubled feelings out. Let's keep on helping him learn to choose appropriate times and places.

There's one particular secret that often enables us to be more successful than we expect. It's *the secret of* CHANNEL-ING *feelings instead of* STOPPING *feelings, remembering that we can actually only stop the act.*

CHOOSING CHANNELS

It's clear by now that outlets for feelings cannot be permitted to flow wildly in every direction. A child may not act them out in any way he wants, nor in any place, nor at any time. There must be limitations put on WHAT he does and WHEN and WHERE.

Fortunately, WHAT he does in one place does not necessarily carry over to all places. It's been found that if a child has one place where he can safely get things out with very few restrictions he behaves better at other times and in other places.

In one nursery school, for instance, a curious thing happened which bears out this point. In the school were certain children who needed particularly concentrated outlets for their aggressions. Each of these children would go upstairs alone with an understanding and acceptant teacher for a time every day or every other day. Here was a playroom with a sturdy table and a chair and a linoleum floor and painted

51

walls that could be washed down. The children did many things here which they could do nowhere else. They smeared the walls with clay. They spilled paint indiscriminately over the floor. They used words that would make grandma's hair rise up straight on her head. Many of them spontaneously called the teacher "mama" and added a string of unmentionable epithets.

The teacher permitted and accepted most of their actions. She put limitations, however, on some. She never allowed a child to hit or kick or otherwise carry out any physical act against her. Nor would she allow any destructiveness which was undesirable or costly. A child could not, for example, take a knife and carve up the table, nor could he throw a toy at the window and break it. But otherwise, he could do things which he could not be permitted to do in the regular nursery schoolrooms downstairs.

The curious part was that, in almost all instances, the need for forbiddings grew considerably less than it had been prior to the sessions upstairs. These children did not long carry the "wilder" type of action over from the upstairs playroom. They themselves seemed to sense that even though such actions were permissible upstairs, downstairs they were not. The two situations were different. Each setup was connected in the children's minds with activities which were appropriate to it. Having gotten things out in a certain time and place, they no longer needed to spill at every moment everywhere.

An interesting little side light was the fact that even though in the upstairs room they had frequently reviled the teacher as "mama," downstairs they *never* attempted this. Of their own accord they were again judging when a thing was appropriate to the time and place and when it was not.

In our homes as well as our regular classrooms there must be due regard not only for what actions are permitted but also for time and place. As in the nursery school cited, children seem to sense where and when their aggression can come out—that is, IF it has been permitted an appropriate time and place in the total course of their lives.

"You can throw rocks outside and pretend that the tree is Rosita, but you can't throw pencils in here at Rosita's head."

"You can't yell smutty words out of the window at all the people who pass by. You can mutter them all you want to in here with me alone."

"You can mess to your heart's content on the linoleum rug but not on the carpet."

"You can talk to me all you want to about your troubles before daddy comes home in the evening, but after that I have to listen to his."

Or, still speaking of appropriate times, a person may be watching a child writhe and yell in a burst of temper, and may think, wisely, *I'll wait till he's a little quieter before I help him choose a different channel. If I tried at this moment he wouldn't hear. Right now, if I can, I'll help him feel I'm loving and acceptant and understanding so he'll be better able when the time comes to show me what's on his mind.*

It is perfectly sound and in order to take the What's and When's and Where's of his action into account and to place limitations on these. The secret all along is to help a child LET OUT THE FEELINGS even though we may need to STOP and RECHANNEL them into DIFFERENT ACTIONS.

Perhaps it does sound confusing. As if the two things were contradictory. But really they aren't.

Take Bob, who is eight, as example. He has packed a toothbrush and shirt and pants into a little old battered bag. With an injured air he opens the door and is about to step from the house into the darkness outside. You come in just in time to see him cast a backward glance as if he were saying, "You'll be sorry that you were so mean." And then you see him square his shoulders with an air that literally mutters, "I'm leaving this house for good and all."

But there's a highway a couple of blocks off where cars streak by and sirens screech every night. For Bob's own safety, his actions must be limited. At the same time, you know that he must also have outlets for his feelings. And so you say, "I can't let you run away, Bob; we'd miss you too much. We want you around here with us. But I know you feel mean-mad. Come on and tell me what's wrong."

Or take five-year-old Mike who is on the way back to school from an excursion to see a steam shovel. Crossing the street, Mike stops in the middle and stalls.

Mike's teacher says, "Get out of the street, Mike; a car's coming."

Mike stands his ground stubbornly.

Quickly the teacher takes Mike by the hand and pulls him firmly onto the sidewalk.

"You dummy," Mike screams.

For two blocks he keeps repeating, "Dumb teacher! Old dummy!"

The teacher mirrors his feelings. "It looks as though you're mad at me, Mike, for having made you do something you didn't want to."

She also shows her acceptance in the good, easy tone of voice which she reinforces by saying, "It's all right for you to show me how you feel."

She makes no effort, however, to stop the outburst, knowing that the "badness" must out and believing that there were no sufficient reasons for trying to postpone it to another time or place. And, true to what usually happens when such procedures are used, Mike is again cheerful by the time the calvalcade reaches school.

We need not let children go willy-nilly into any actions they wish. Nor do we need to go into any actions they wish us to.

Cynthia, fourteen, wants her mother to climb down at once from the top of a ladder where she is perched straightening the china on the highest cupboard shelf. "Come on, Mo-ther, and fix my hair."

"Not now, not until I've finished. Can't you see I'm busy?"

"But why not?" the anger rising.

"I know you're sore. But not *now*."

"Oh, you . . ." Cynthia growls.

In spite of herself, mother feels anger rising inside her. "Run along, Cynthia. Not *now!*"

"You're an old bag!" shouts Cynthia.

Mother is about to shout back. But suddenly she remembers. "I got mad, dear. And you did too!"

Just a simple reflection with sudden acceptance not only of Cynthia's mood but her own as well. Cynthia smiles behind her mutterings and then says suddenly, "Gee, Mom, can't I help?"

As a final case in point, let's go back to our Heinie who wouldn't eat and who had threatened to fling his food all around. His father had noticed his anger and had reflected it. He had given Heinie a chance to bring some of his resentful feelings out. Suppose now that Heinie actually begins to throw his food. This obviously won't do. It's destructive to the rug and furniture, and, besides, a chicken bone might land in father's eye. Heinie's father is now in this spot: How can he continue to accept and mirror Heinie's feelings and yet at the same time curb Heinie's actions?

Here is father's opportunity to slip back into the good old ways of disciplining. He is, in fact, on the verge of this. He feels anger mounting inside him and he starts to think longingly of every threat in his vocabulary, from lambasting Heinie to forbidding him ice-cream cones for a week. But he, too, remembers the new ways of discipline just in time:

SEE how he feels.
ACCEPT how he feels.
REFLECT how he feels.

Help him GET OUT THE POISON.
If necessary, help him
STEER his ACTIONS.

"Heinie," father says, his anger dwindling, "you're mad at me. It's not hard to see that. Why don't you tell me about it? You can say anything you feel like saying. It's okay to get out your anger in words. But I can't let you throw food around. Understand?"

Heinie looks up challengingly. "Suppose I do it anyway?"

Heinie's father notices quickly that there has already been a change in Heinie. He is no longer concentrating on throwing the food. He is focused on threatening his father. In other words, Heinie is now using threats instead of food-flinging as a way of releasing his anger. This is the feeling that his father now mirrors.

"You want to threaten me, Heinie!"

"I sure do. You're an old meanie. I'd like you to trip in the garden and get mud in your mouth. Old stinky mud. Old stinky . . . *nice* daddy!" And Heinie bursts into a wide grin. "Come on, Dad, let's play kick-ball. I'll eat this here stuff up first real fast!"

The crisis is past!

"But!" you protest, "it doesn't work that way. If I'd forbidden him, my child would have gone right on throwing the food. I'd have had to resort to punishment, I know. The mere forbidding wouldn't have helped."

Heinie's father had not, however, used *mere forbidding*. He had forbidden the action only. He had not forbidden the feeling. He had given Heinie's feelings many chances to come out. He continued to give them an OUT. The curtailment lay in the fact that they could not come out in this particular *kind of action*. If they had needed to come out further, *they would have to be channeled into other kinds of action* instead.

56

It is clear by now that a child must endanger neither himself nor others by actions of any sort if this can possibly be prevented. It is obvious that he must not be destructive. For if he destroys or hurts, he not only does harm to what he destroys or hurts, he also does harm to himself. He frightens himself and sometimes so greatly that life becomes too heavy and dark.

It's our job to help children channel the outlets. It's our job to help children handle their feelings. As long as, and in so far as, we ignore or deny that a child has troubled feelings, or fearful or mean ones, we desert him. We leave him to handle them all by himself.

And this is too hard.

It's too much for a child to be left to handle his feelings alone. It's too big a task to require of him. It's difficult enough, goodness knows, for us when we help him. We don't always do such a perfect job. So why expect him in his immaturity to do more than can we who are grown up?

When we focus on his actions alone as we ordinarily do when we try to change what he does, we are virtually saying, "I don't care how you feel. All I care about is how you behave. You'll have to take care of the feelings by yourself!"

If he tries to tell us of the "bad" and sometimes terrifying feelings inside him, we tell him in return that we will have none of them. We leave him desolate and deserted to find his own way of release.

He is desperate, and chooses knives perhaps, and guns and gang warfare. He is grim, and perhaps hits out at Negroes or Jews, at Mexicans or Catholics. "You rotten nigger" may be an epithet which, if properly disrobed of its disguise, might mean, "You rotten father." He grows miserable, and perhaps uses his own body as a "whipping boy," getting asthma, hay fever, hives or a cough by which to cough up what he can not say. Or he finds some other behavior problem to serve as outlet. In any case, two things happen: He *must* find some outlet for his "bad" feelings. He must choose this all alone, unaware and helpless, deserted by us where he needs us most.

Our children need help in diverting their feelings into new grooves. It is our job to help and encourage the outflow through safe channels instead of through harmful and dangerous ones.

"You feel mean, I know. You can tell me, dear, how you feel!"

Or, "You can show me."

"You mean I can say or do anything?" our unbeliever counters.

"As long as it isn't destructive or dangerous. And I'm here to help you decide if it is."

As we do this sort of defining and as we follow the various steps that have been laid down, we discover that disciplining a child isn't so heavy. In contrast to the old way of grimness, we may find that the new way possesses new strengths and new fun.

STATING SIMPLE RULES SIMPLY

In spite of all the foregoing, we may still be looking for an over-all rule-giving solution to disciplinary ills. Just as the city traffic bureau looks to signposts to eliminate all violations!

Yes, rules are in order. But they help most when a child feels over and above regulations that he is accepted and understood. Then he *wants* to obey far more than he otherwise would.

Rules are sometimes heeded better when they are stated succinctly and impersonally, like simple truths rather than like personally tinged whims.

What do we mean by rules impersonally stated?

"It's time for bed" goes over better with a small child than "You've got to go to bed now." "Up goes the shirt, right over the head!" gains more willing response than does the direct
58

command that tells him, "Take your shirt off fast." "Bedtime's at eight," in its turn, goes over better with an older youngster than ordering and arguing and explaining nightly.

"No movie on school nights!" The rule stands there firmly.

But this is not all. There is one more step. And this is the most important one in getting the rule to work: *We must let our child "gripe" about it to his heart's content. We must*

Father: "Come on now, Butch, hop into bed."
Son: "But sleeping's such a waste of time, Daddy!"

remember he is bound to be resentful over having this rule imposed on him.

We'll expect the protests and will accept them. These have to do with feelings. The rule has to do only with how a child acts. "I know you hate going to bed." . . . "You feel abused and angry not to get to the show!" He doesn't want to obey and yet he has to. He naturally *feels* mean. And he must let the protest come out. If it doesn't come out in words, it will come out in some other way.

"Rules never work by themselves in our house," argued

one mother. "We need to reinforce them with good hard punishments," said another. "Otherwise Buck doesn't listen. . . ."

Two months later their stories were different. Said the first, "When I tried the rules along with the release and acceptance of angry feelings, the rules *did* work. I realize now it's one thing to give rules and insist on a certain kind of action, and then *not* let a child even *say* he hates you for it. It's quite another thing if you permit his feelings to come out all along and if you respect them. He begins to respect the rules."

Said the other mother, "Buck listens to me now because I listen to him. He doesn't have to duck what I say because I don't try to duck how he feels. His father doesn't either. His dad tells him, 'I know how you feel, Buck. I know you don't like our not letting you have the car at night. I used to feel the same way!' You can just see that his dad is *with* Buck —getting his own youth back. Buck swears like a trooper but he hasn't done fifty-nine other aggravating things to get even with us for not giving in on the car."

In every person's life there are you-must-do-it *musts*. Even so, "Come on, guy, the doctor has to give you the shot" is ordinarily more effective than saying, "Sit down and take it." At such times, a child may need to be held. The frightening effect can be softened by not forgetting to bring in the fact that we do understand how our child feels even though we must insist that this thing be seen through. "You don't like it, Pete, but it's got to be done!" . . . "It hurts, I know, but let's get it over with!" . . . "You feel like murdering me for doing this. But here goes . . . Now we're through!" Here, again, we need to let a child "get even" and complain and gripe and scold all he wants.

Nonetheless, we can take comfort in knowing that in the long run resistance will be lessened when we have disciplined according to the principles and procedures that this book recounts.

60

Right now, though, since these new ways of discipline are so strange, we may feel that we're in a topsy-turvy land where everything's as crazy as the Mad Hatter.

"But why," we keep questioning, "why focus on the negative feelings? These are the very emotions we want our children to forget."

And yet we already know the answer. The negative feelings are the very ones we don't want a child to lose sight of as long as they hurt or press or drive him to disturbing behavior. For then these emotions will move out of view and out of hand. They may slip into the un-get-at-able, shut up in the unconscious mind beyond will and control.

We may feel that accepting the negative feelings—the angry ones especially—encourages them and fixes them. "Won't a child get the habit? Won't he stay mad all the time?"

Quite the reverse. At first, in his newly found chance to bring out his anger, a child may do it to excess. For a while he may even grow worse. But then, almost invariably, he finds a balance, the meanness lessens and the gladness comes. The more he releases the anger, the less of it will remain, PROVIDED it has been handled in an acceptant way that doesn't make new anger take the place of what has drained off.

"Won't he be mean, though, to the neighbors and rude to everyone if we at home accept such things?"

Ordinarily, the reverse holds true. (Remember, after he has had sufficient outlets he usually manages to handle the Where's and When's.) The more his meanness and his rudeness can come out and be understood and accepted, the less pushed a child will feel to explode here, there and everywhere.

Ordinarily, too, as we help him meet and work through his feelings, a new confidence and closeness grows between us.

This is what happened to five-year-old Billy who let out his bothers at the rate of a mile a minute while his father listened. Billy's father, however, did not scold or lecture or try to explain. On the contrary, he knew that when enough of the "badness" was out, the "goodness" would have a chance to move into its rightful place. And so he waited and mirrored Billy's feelings, permissively accepting a good deal of abuse. Finally, the bitterness and storm passed, and Billy, beaming and grateful, put his hand on his dad's knee and murmured, "Gee, Daddy. I love you. I love you as much as twenty donkeys and a junk yard full of dog-do. You're the best daddy in the world."

We need not fear that we are putting ideas in the heads of these children. We are merely accepting ideas that are already there. We are helping these diminish as we follow the leads which the child himself brings.

But if we are to do this for a child, we will need to remain acceptant and loving and really *with* him. Following the outlined procedures mechanically won't work. Our children have troubles, as great to them and as distressing as our adult troubles are to us. The more we can appreciate their *real* feelings and really feel with them, the more we will find our disciplinary troubles decreasing. It isn't enough to get the new ways of discipline in our heads. It's necessary to feel *with* and *for* a child in our hearts. We will need to go back again and again to our very first rule: Listen so as to hear; watch so as to see; and feel what he feels as as best we can.

6. Dispelling disobedience

As we think about discipline our minds invariably return again and again to questions about the old stand-bys. How about punishments? Rewards? Isolating a child? Ignoring him? Reasoning? Explaining? All the various things we've tried in the past? Can't the new discipline dress up these old things and give them a new look? Then we'd feel more secure since we'd be treading at least on familiar ground.

How about rewards?

"If you don't wet your bed, Sonny, we'll paste a gold star on this chart." . . . "If you act like a big, brave boy when you go to the doctor, we'll buy you an ice-cream cone." . . . "If you are nice to sister, we'll take you to a show." . . . "If you stop being lazy and work hard at school, we'll get you a motor bike."

Let's take a good, long look at what we are actually doing. For one thing, by our very own words we are showing a child that we expect him to "do wrong." "If you don't wet your bed" means that we think he will. "If you act like a brave boy" implies that we think he won't. "If you're nice to sister" . . . "If you stop being lazy" show him that we expect him to be just what we tell him not to be. What we are saying is really this: "I don't have confidence in you. I know you're going to be bad."

63

"I'd hate to disappoint her," says fifteen-year-old Andy, shrugging his shoulders. "Anyway, I get what I want by keeping her thinking I'll be bad. Of course, I have to be bad often enough to convince her that she's not paying me for nothing. And it makes her raise the ante every so often, too."

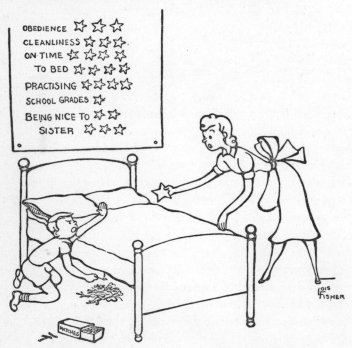

"Don't hand me that old stuff, Mom. It's worth a thousand *dollars* for me not to do *this*."

To children, rewards are a kind of bribe. To Andy they were, as they are to others, the profit in the bargain. They were barter. He was exchanging "goodness" for the material gains he would receive and then using "badness" to raise the market price.

As the bargaining progresses, we find ourselves having to offer more and more.

Bribes and *promises* are no more than a promissory note to pay. They follow the same principles as do rewards and are no more effective.

"I've tried making promises and giving rewards of many sorts," says one mother. "They're all alike. They work for a while and then they're no longer effective. My child seems to lose interest. He wants bigger and better ones. He wants more and more."

Sometimes we may choose to use rewards anyway as quick, temporary boosters. But if we rely on the reward to accomplish everything for us, we cheat a child of what he is really after. We fail to give him the values he really seeks. He wants our love, our appreciation and our recognition for what he does in the same way that we ourselves want recognition—by another's valuing the real worth of our accomplishment and the effort we put into the doing. He wants our acceptance of what he really is, our understanding of his true feelings—the bad as well as the good. We are failing him by paying him in dross.

When he does things and acts in ways that make us feel appreciative, then sharing our appreciation with him—this is another and far better sort of reward. "Thanks, dear, for being quiet this afternoon. It was such a help. It saved me so much time; I got my work done twice as fast. . . ."

Then, if we are in the mood, we can share the resulting leisure time together in an outing or a game or a show. This, too, is a kind of reward. The best part, however, lies in the good feelings between us. These are worth a thousand gold stars.

Says Curley, six, whose mother had been thinking that gold stars were at the bottom of his keeping his bed dry, "Suppose you don't bother to paste them on any more, Ma. The thing I really like is that you've been so pretty and nice."

The change in her attitude was what counted. The stars had not mattered at all.

How about praise?

Praise can be one thing or another. It can be a sincere expression of appreciation. Or it can be used like rewards and bribes as a means of buying what one wants. In the first instance it rises sincerely from within; in the second it is artificially put on.

Unfortunately, praise is usually a kind of outer shell for the inner value. "She puts on the fine words outside," says ten-year-old Mort, "but inside her face is turned away."

Superficial *praise* or pats on the back won't do it. They are just another sort of gold star. What a child needs and wants are the loving feelings in us that are deep and honest and good.

How about punishments?

"You can't let a child get away with murder. He has to be made to suffer when he's misbehaved." But let's remember: A child misbehaves because he has suffered, because he is hurt or afraid. By punishing we add insult to injury. Then, the healthier he is, the more he will fight back. He will become worse unless we make the punishment so hard that it destroys his "gumption" and leaves him weak and defeated, as if there were no use in doing anything but give up and hide.

"I have to spank you, Don, much as I hate to. I've told you fifty-nine times never to cross the street alone, and yet you persist. I *have* to do something to make you remember." . . . "I'm sorry, Mary, but I do have to take away your privileges. You've been abusing them and I *have* to make you see it's no use your staying out till twelve when your mother and I have been lenient enough to say eleven."

"I have to make you remember. . . ." This is reechoed many times over. We infer that punishment makes a child keep in mind the disagreeable consequences which follow an act that to him was pleasant. We expect that he will automatically connect the punishment with the crime.

But he doesn't. As we read in the opening pages of this

66

book, a child most often separates them. He remembers the pleasant act as pleasant. He remembers his mother or father or teacher as a disagreeable kill-joy. He thinks, "Now when I do this next time I'll have to see that I'm not found out." Or he ponders and broods on the cruelty of his elders and gets to feeling meaner than mean.

As we look back on our own childhood, can we recall exactly what we were punished for? Very seldom. We remember more readily the punisher and the punishment and sometimes also the resentment that accrued. "I hated to be put in the closet. I can't remember for the life of me, though, what it was for."

"I hated to be put in the closet" translated into unconscious emotional language usually means "I hated the person who put me into the closet." This is in truth what our children do.

"What did your father spank you for, Roddy?"

"I don't remember," came the eight-year-old's answer. "All I know is I hate his guts."

We need to stop again and take stock. What are we after if not to gain a child's cooperation and good will, knowing that then obedience will come more readily. It's easy to see that cooperation is bound to dwindle when punishment increases a child's resentments.

Still another point is worth mentioning here. Some parents boast about never spanking a child in anger. They pride themselves on keeping their tempers and patience while they pronounce a dire penalty. "That," says seventeen-year-old Frances, "makes me madder than anything else. They act one way and feel another. The old hypocrites. It's rank insincerity, that's all."

There is nothing more defeating than cruelty meted out as kindness or than anger clothed as love.

It's quite natural that we should be angry, annoyed, put out by some of the things our children do. We're bound to be. Then why not show it?

"I am angry. I don't like what you're doing." . . . "It scares me when you cross the street and I get real mad." Or a simple statement: "Look, I don't like that," with rounded and wholesome anger in our voices. At least this is *real* and *sincere*. It's far better punishment than the put-on air of patient martyrdom while we wield the big stick.

Our children know then that we mean what we're saying. They know that we are being honest with them. They know that we are human and that we care about them enough to get ruffled by them.

Of course, if the outbursts of anger are so frequent as to overshadow the loving moments, we may recognize that we ourselves need to have help in understanding why we feel as we do.

How about isolation?

Isn't that a good thing either?

We say to a youngster, "You sit there in the corner and don't budge. And don't you let me hear a word out of you. Just keep quiet a while and think about how you're supposed to act."

Meanwhile we know as well as he does what sort of thoughts he's thinking. Only we're doing nothing to help him handle them. In leaving him alone by himself in the corner we're again leaving him to handle his feelings alone. Again this makes the hurt and fear and anger in him grow worse. In turn, he has a harder time accepting what we offer him of our love.

How about reasoning with a child?
How about explaining things to him?

Aren't reasoning and explaining good ways?

"Go on and tell me what I'm deprived of and quit the talk,"

says thirteen-year-old Blanding. Five-year-old Betty quite simply put her hands over her ears.

"My eight-year-old took me down a peg," recounted Charlene's mother. "I used all my persuasiveness. I explained on and on, reasoning with her about how important it was for her to tell the truth. I thought I'd just clinched the point when I noticed her sniffing. 'Oh, Mom,' she exclaimed. 'Isn't that the most delicious smell of bacon next door?' Did I feel cheap! Her mind had simply gone wandering away from my very best words."

The constant reasoning can run along like water trickling, either making no impression or wearing a person down. And far too often another element intrudes itself into the reasoning—the element of *threat*.

Marina, nine, started out in life expressing her resentment directly to her mother in a healthy, outright manner. At five she yelled, "I wish you'd go way and die and never bother me any more."

"Marina, you shouldn't say things like that. People will hear you and think you aren't a nice girl. Don't you know we don't talk that way to our parents? We respect them, dear!" . . .

"Marina, don't you realize your mother is a wonderful mother? If you talk that way and something really happened to her, imagine how you'd feel. You'd never forgive yourself." . . .

"Marina, you must not say such things. You hurt your mother's feelings. And she does so much for you. If you keep on hurting her she might not love you anymore."

Such talk ran on and on. Marina's parents used *reasoning* as their method. They reasoned and reasoned, all very logically. Inadvertently, though, behind their tempered words, threats crept in. "You'll be sorry if you lose your mother . . ." "You'll be sorry because she won't love you anymore."

69

As the talk-talk-talk went on and on, it wore Marina down. She tried to answer but couldn't. The big people around her talked so much faster and so much more adroitly than she. She felt defeated. Finally, she closed her ears and she closed her mouth. She choked down the angry words that rose inside her.

But now, at nine, the anger was coming out through her mouth in another fashion. It was coming out in continuous lies. The lies were substituting for the earlier aggression. They were simply another way of letting the anger out.

Explaining and reasoning, threatening and talking on and on are little better than punishing. In fact, they may be worse. They last longer. They wear a child down.

Says Jerry, three and a half,

> I've got a lot of people,
> Great big people,
> And they sit and they sit all around.
>
> They've got great big faces
> And great big mouthies
> And they give me a pain
> 'Cause they talk and talk.

Ten-year-old Kenny's mother was also one of those talkers who reasoned and explained on and on. Kenny, with beautiful clarity, shows how, because of this, she has robbed him of chances to share his troubles with her. He shows, too, how she incidentally has robbed herself of closeness that would have helped no end in making Kenny's disciplinary problems decrease. Kenny says, "I wish I could . . . *but* . . . I can't tell my mother my bothers. Because when I do, she uses up all my time explaining and explaining why she had to do what she did and why I shouldn't."

Constant talk and reasoning takes the problem away from the child. We take it into our hands, or rather into our mouths. We do all the thinking about it. We express ourselves concerning it but we don't give our child a chance to express himself.

Instead, we need to give him the opportunities to tell us and show us how he is thinking and feeling so that we may help him work these things through. This takes us right back to where we started from. It takes us back to the importance of accepting his feelings no matter how "bad" they are.

HE STILL NEEDS TO LEARN SELF-CONTROL

"Oh," we may sigh. "Here we are again. Back at license. Back at letting his 'bad' feelings run on. How will he ever learn self-control?"

As we said in the last chapter, we need to differentiate between his actions and his feelings. We can forbid certain actions and possibly stop them. From this we gather that feelings follow the same pattern. Only they don't.

We forbid a child, for instance, to hit the baby. If he stops hitting we say, "The actions are stopped. They are *under control.*"

But if we forbid the feelings, they don't stop. He still feels like hitting the baby. If he doesn't in some way get his feelings out now while he is still freshly aware of them, they may go into his unconscious mind where he is not aware of them and reappear, unconsciously aimed at new targets as he grows. He may hit out at younger children in school, or at his junior partner in business, or at his partner in married life. His undercover feelings may come out in intolerance and prejudice, in crime or in war. The original form lies hidden, but the feelings themselves are not *stopped.* Unfortunately, he can no longer stop them. He no longer knows what they are. They are completely *out of his control.*

When we fail to help a child release his feelings, when we handle him so that he denies them and pushes them into his unconscious mind, they move out of his control. He becomes

71

blind to them. He can no longer see them. He can do nothing about them.

Could we fix a broken bowl if some of the pieces were invisible to us?

Could we bind a wound and make it well if we couldn't see it?

Quite apparently we do not want to cause our children to become blind to a thing which they need so desperately to handle. We do not want to make them take feelings that press at them and put these out of awareness. For if we do this, we put their feelings out of their control.

Self-control lies in the other direction. It lies in keeping the "bad" feelings in the open until they work themselves out. It lies in helping children learn to direct their feelings into unhurtful and harmless channels. *Learning to channelize is learning to control.* For then they steer their feelings. Then they do control their emotions. By *directing* the type of expression; not by denying what exists.

LEARNING TO CONFORM TO SOCIETY

In spite of all these considerations, when parents and teachers first encounter the principles that we have been discussing they are apt to keep on insisting: "But a child must learn the ways of our culture. He must have restraints imposed upon him. He has to learn to do as others do and not stand out like a sore thumb."

Certainly a child must learn to conform. Helping him to do so is a part of discipline. But it is not the whole thing. We want him to acquire certain patterns in conformity with customs and the demands of society, but we don't want him so hemmed in by these that he is fearful of being creative and of progressing as he grows. We don't want him to be so set in the patterns he develops that he fails to change as the world about him changes. We don't want him to be so bound that he can not take his part in helping to change society, to

72

weed out its ills and put it into better shape. We don't want him to be like the little old woman who was so rigidly committed to the ways of her fathers that she did all her stitching by hand and scoffed at the sewing machine.

An individual needs to be free enough to try new ways and new methods, to experiment, to explore. To teach a child to *mind* for the sole sake of minding is teaching him to accept, unquestioningly, the word of authority. We prepare him to follow—to follow without thought of why he does what he does. He needs to have confidence in himself which enables him to meet new conditions as they arise, to adjust to new things as they come to him, to develop and move ahead.

However, unless he learns to consider the existing patterns and to conform in appropriate ways as he grows, he will have an unnecessarily difficult time. A lot of energy which could be spent more creatively will be spent in useless and wasteful directions. If he learns appropriate conformities, he is freed to give himself over to bigger and better things. A person brought up to the small conventionalities labeled "good manners" will be freer, for instance, at a dinner party to exchange points of view and enjoy other people than one who spends all his energy watching his hostess to see what to do.

As a child grows he learns conformities gradually, just as he learns arithmetic. We don't expect him to do trigonometry at six, although he can accomplish the simple adding of two pennies to two. When he starts to write we accept his scrawly print and beam in spite of the imperfections. We smile when he turns a letter around backward or makes it upside down. He's so little, we think, and are proud of his spontaneous attempts to ape what we older ones do. We smile, too, as he mimics our walk, our talk, our gestures, our facial expressions, and later as he wants to imitate and dress like us and be big like us and do as we do.

All along he learns these conformities gradually without any pushing or prodding from us. He imitates this or that as

73

his mind and muscles are ready to pick it up. Because he loves us. Because he wants to be like us. We don't have to insist on these things at all.

In the same manner he will spontaneously learn many of the things we feel we must insist on, if only we give him time to grow into them. But no, we can't wait. "He must learn cleanliness," we say, for example, and so he will, by fits and starts and in due course of time unless we press him so much that he grows negative. Most little boys proudly imitate daddy in standing up to urinate. They do this quite of their own accord. We don't have to insist that this is what custom demands.

What a child hears, what he sees, what he absorbs, what he feels—all make an impact. HE LEARNS MANY THINGS ABOUT BEING GOOD THAT WE DON'T HAVE TO TELL HIM. He learns them through contact and closeness with others as he grows.

We don't sit a child down in front of us and try to hammer in the big essential rules of ethics that make a person good. We don't, for instance, have to reason with him by the hour that he must not take human life. We don't say, "He has to learn such things, so we must tell him!" We know he learns them from all around him. Most children do not need to be told that they must not steal; they absorb it automatically from what they see and hear. Most children need not be specifically told that murder is outside the law; they absorb this too.

Nor do we have to sit children down to hammer in the lesser rules and precepts. We can trust far more than we ordinarily do that they will absorb these as they become ready to. We don't have to say anything to a twelve-year-old son who scoffs at girls. When he's nineteen he's apt to be the epitome of graciousness anyway. We don't have to lecture a ten-year-old daughter about her lack of manners. At fifteen we will probably find her poring over Emily Post. We may prod and preach about a youngster's lack of ideals

74

only to find, a few years later, that his head is in the clouds and is full of the highest dreams.

We can do more harm than good by demanding too much or too strenuously. As long as we fight him, he'll fight us. As long as we argue with him, he'll argue back. As long as we yell at him, he'll yell too. As long as we boss, he'll try to boss us.

Says the mother of thirteen-year-old Roy every evening, "You come to dinner *fast* . . . Don't you dare keep us waiting or we won't wait."

Says Roy every morning, "You fix my lunch *fast* . . . Don't you dare keep me waiting. If you do, I won't wait."

Our insistence begets counterinsistence; our aggression engenders counteraggression. Or else we may make our children grow far too strict with themselves. That part of them which we call their conscience turns into another parent inside them which beats them down. It can force them to duplicate so exactly what we believe that they fail to find themselves or discover their own essential beliefs.

Most parents feel that they do have to insist on a certain amount of conformity in their homes for the common convenience of all concerned. "I can't have a football game under my window when I'm doing the monthly accounts." . . . "I can't have the radio blaring when the baby's going to sleep." . . . "I can't keep heating up food all evening while one straggler after another straggles in." . . . But even seemingly essential requests may perhaps seem unessential when reexamined with the child's nature and needs in mind.

"I found I was leveling so many demands at my children that a regular refusal-pattern resulted, half to protect themselves and half to get back at me and make me mad. So I figured, 'Why fight? Over mealtimes, for instance? They're big enough to serve up their own food.' So I began fixing a one-dish dinner that I left in the oven for them to dig into when they came in. And I gave them the choice of either being on time or of serving themselves. Most evenings they chose to come on time so they could eat with us. When they chose to stay out, that was all right. We just didn't fuss."

Certain things bother some of us more than others. One mother literally cringes at mud being tracked in. Another hardly sees it. Said the one who did mind, "Look, boys! This is a peculiarity of mine! I know I'm an idiot to mind it so much. And yet I do. So have a heart, won't you?"

" 'You're a pest!' they laughed. But they did what I asked. They wouldn't have, though, six months earlier. At that time I was insisting on so *many* things that another request would only have added more anger to what was already there."

We need to repeat:

IF A CHILD IS A PERSISTENTLY "BAD" CHILD,
HE IS A HURT CHILD.
He is a fearful child.
He is a child choking with anger.

Even though we were never aware of it, we may somehow have deprived him. Even though we never saw it, we may have left certain of his emotional wants unnourished. Even though we do not see why, he may still hold resentment inside him and be bringing this out.

We don't know why he has been hurt. We don't know why he has been frightened. We don't know what he is angry about. All we know is that he is not behaving as we would like to have him.

At this point we need to turn a searchlight on ourselves with great honesty. Perhaps we are so involved in preconceived notions of what we would like him to be that we are losing sight of what he himself is. Perhaps we are not recognizing things that are of importance to *him* as an individual in his own right. Things he needs but may not himself be aware of. Things he is not able to tell us about. Perhaps we

76

will need to readjust our sights and change ourselves as well as him.

In any case, we will need to have patience with ourselves. After all, we are learning a new language. We can't expect to turn the page and all of a sudden turn ourselves over to completely new ways.

If we try and try and don't succeed and want to, then we are wise if we seek professional help.

MEETING HIM VS. MAKING HIM

For years now we have been asking: *What can we do to* make *him obey?*

We have tried for the past goodness-knows-how-long to *make* him. . . . We've reasoned until we're blue in the face . . . but that hasn't worked. We've punished until he's black and blue somewhere else . . . but that hasn't worked. We've punished and threatened. We've given rewards and promises. We've appealed to reason and have explained on and on. . . . But—nine chances in ten—*none of these things have worked.*

If they have worked, the results probably haven't lasted more than a day or a week.

Ordinarily, as long as we keep on trying to MAKE a child do this or that, he'll try to go us one better and not do it.

Says twelve-year-old Louise, with irritation quite apparent, "My mother thinks she's so smart the way she tries to get around me. She spends her days scheming how she can make me do what she wants. Well, *I* don't have to scheme. I know how to get around her. She thinks *she's* so big. Well, she's not."

If the tenth chance has fallen to us and the old ways seem to have worked, there is still the possibility that another problem will have entered as a substitute for the first. It is true that a child may get over misbehavior as we handle it in the older ways. There is that tenth chance that we can

77

make him get over acting in an undesirable manner by punishing or by pushing and prodding him until he finally gives up his misbehavior in sheer self-protection. But as long as the feelings that drove him into the disturbing behavior are there, he isn't safe. *He simply gets over one problem to have another problem take its place.* The second problem may be less "naughty" or less noticeable, but it disturbs him all the same.

One child is "cured" of thumb-sucking but develops a stutter. Another is punished out of arguing but develops a cough. A third, at eight, is made to stop having temper tantrums. At eighteen she is detached and remote. "I can't make contact with anyone," she complains. "I'm unutterably lonely and alone!"

No matter how subtly the idea of MAKING a child enters the picture, no matter how carefully we try to hide it, he'll see it and sense it. He may give up and choose another outlet for his feelings—a substitute one for the first. But ordinarily, if he is sturdy and healthy in his drive for independence, he will fight by fair means or foul. He WON'T be MADE to do things. For if he is, he will be giving up his birthright—his right to grow into a thinking, productive, creative adult.

When we examine the total load of our requests and requirements, we may be astonished. "Why, if I were told to do half as many things as my kid and forbidden to do as many others," remarked one father, "I'd move out so fast you wouldn't even see the dust. It's not only that I'd rebel. It's also that I wouldn't want to lose every ounce of confidence I had in myself by having no say on my own."

The discipline which fosters his best sort of adjustment is the discipline that leads him to complete himself and yet *want* to consider others, to exert self-control and to conform in appropriate ways as he grows.

We will, of necessity, give him good patterns to imitate. We will give him simple suggestions, rules stated simply without pushing or overaggression on our part to beget pulling and counteraggression from him. We won't ask him too early to do things he cannot do comfortably, for then he will feel defeated in gaining a good inner sense of achievement. We'll leave till later whatever he is not neuromuscularly ready for—whatever his body or his mind is too immature to accomplish. We will be careful not to pile too many demands on him all at once, knowing how hard it is even for us who are grown to learn a host of things all together. And, most important, we will take his feelings into account, realizing that he is no automaton or puppet whose strings we can pull to bring a performance about.

With most of us the hardest task, as we try out the new ways of discipline, will have to do with helping a child work through those angry, "mean" feelings that none of us like to face. And yet—as we see now—this is of paramount importance, not only for his sake, but for the sake of others.

We do well to repeat four essential points here:

Let's—

Help a child LIQUIDATE HIS ANGER
as it arises.

Let's—

Help him liquidate it in
UNHURTFUL AND HARMLESS WAYS.

Let's—

Help him direct it AGAINST THE
PERSON OR PERSONS WHO ACTUALLY PRODUCE IT.

And remember—

Let's—

NOT try to CHANGE the "MEAN" FEELINGS
into NICE ones.

LOVING FEELINGS come best after the mean ones have
worn themselves out.

YOU CAN COUNT ON WHAT HE HAS IN HIM

Too often we fail to realize that we have an important ally *inside* our child. He isn't all badness. He isn't all disobedience. He isn't just a bundle of antisocial, asocial, unsocial impulses. There are powerful forces at work in him that keep him striving to complete himself, to be himself, to find himself and to find others; to live with them and among them and to give and share.

In the normal course of living if all is normal—in spite of moments of badness—we won't have to do drastic things to make a child good. As he grows he gradually finds that his achievements count more to him when they not only complete him but contribute to others, and that pleasure and warmth and beauty mean more when the relishing of them is not his alone. He finds as he works with others that he becomes one with them and that brooding isolation vanishes. He feels himself more soundly and vitally belonging to and connected with a common life force.

As he passes through the days of living, he opens his ears and hears the precepts and rules and laws of the land and the ways of the culture in which he lives. He sees how people act and he absorbs what is considered right and wrong. Essentially, he wants to conform and abide in order to belong and to be accepted. He wants to please us. He wants to do what is considered good and right so that his achievement may be valued and recognized. He wants to measure up and be a worthy, worth-while person, to give pleasure to others and to give love as a part of being more deeply loved.

The more confidence a child has in himself, the more capable will he feel in learning what he needs to know about conforming to the ways of the world about him. The more confidence a child has in us and the more of friendship he feels between us, the more will he want to imitate our ways as he grows. With confidence in himself and confidence in us, he learns to conform—not by being pushed and prodded,
80

but by his own earnest wish and a feeling that, now he is ready, he can do these things. Our confidence in him nourishes his confidence both in us and in himself.

We *can* have confidence in him. For there is a propulsion in every human being to fulfill himself in the deepest, richest and soundest way that he can. If only he is not beaten back too unmercifully. If only he is not too defeated. If only he is not hurt so much and made so afraid and angry that his real potentialities cannot get through.

Part Two

Handling crucial moments as he grows

7. Better beginnings

Important Notice. This chapter is not only about babies and small children. It's about ALL OF US. It's about your children NO MATTER HOW OLD THEY ARE! It's about your parents' child too!

So— Don't say, "This doesn't concern me. My child's older so I'll skip this part of the book and not read about the first years."

IF you are to handle discipline well, knowing about the first years is a *must*. All parents and teachers should know about these first years in order to understand their children— no matter how old they are now.

This is why: there's a child part in every one of us. If we could take this child part out from our unconscious mind and look it over, we'd notice that it had some characteristics of the tiny infant, some characteristics of the toddling youngster, some characteristics belonging to this or that crucial phase of the earliest years.

The child part, although hidden in the unconscious, makes its appearance in many ways. Sometimes it shows in an adult in "nice child" behavior; sometimes in behavior of a more "brattish" sort.

Most of us like to "snuggle" close to another person and feel that we are being warmly "cuddled." That's still the baby in us, and a very nice part to have! Many of us still get a queer sort of enjoyment out of picking ears or noses. That's still the small child in us and a part we condemn. When an ingénue talks like a sweet little thing of three, it's the baby part and very attractive. But when she gets to be forty, the baby part isn't so charming any more.

Many times the child part that persists is an *unfinished* part. The baby or small youngster never finished living it out

Mother: "But it's not *time* for him to be hungry!"

to his satisfaction. And so, with a kind of hidden insistence, it continues on.

When an eight-year-old sucks his thumb, a baby part in him is still performing because it has never been satisfied. For some reason he didn't get enough sucking when he was tiny and so he sucks now. Perhaps when he grows older he changes to sucking on wads of gum, or more acceptably, to sucking at the stem of a mellow pipe! But it's all one and the same thing. The baby part in him is expressing an unfinished, unsatisfied need.

86

The clinging vine may be the girl who didn't have enough chance to cling and receive love earlier. The silent lad may be the boy whose baby cries went unheard so that he still feels that he can't achieve communication and unconsciously figures, "Why bother?" The man who pushes into the center of a crowd and demands attention may still be seeking the belonging that went unsatisfied in his first years. The perpetual nibbler may still be expressing an unsatisfied yearning to eat when hungry rather than at scheduled times.

In the child of five or ten, in the youth of fifteen or twenty, and in the adult of thirty or fifty, there lodge remnants of a child part that began during the first years of life. *The facets of this child-part are more easily managed if we understand how they began.* As we gain a picture of them and a sense of their realness, we gain also deeper acceptance of the person in whom they persist. Then we're in a better position to help him work out the unwanted feelings so that his behavior can change.

And so—

If you have a new baby or are about to have one, you'll want to read this chapter to see how to prevent disciplinary problems from taking root . . .

If you have an older child, you will want to read it as a basis for handling his discipline now . . .

If you're a teacher, you will want to read it, because you too must deal with the baby parts which many of your children carry into the schoolroom and devil you with. . . .

But before you read further, here's one more word for you IF YOU'RE THE PARENT OF A CHILD PAST FOUR OR FIVE: You've got a hard job ahead. You're going to read about things you've done and which can't, you'll think, be undone. You're going to read about how you might have done them far better. Most probably you'll have one of two reactions. For one, you may become defensive and say, "These new-fangled

87

notions. I still believe in the good old ways!" Or you may begin to berate yourself, condemning yourself roundly for having irreparably injured your child by the wrong methods you used.

Neither of these attitudes will, however, be helpful. There's another that's better. "Look," you can say to yourself, "I didn't know these things when my child was small. There was no way of my dreaming that what I was doing wasn't best for him. In fact, I was advised to do what I did. I stuck to the letter of the law. I shouldn't blame myself now. What I should do is try to pick up the pieces."

Fortunately, with acceptance and love and a real desire to make up for past mistakes, many fine things can happen. And so you can say to yourself, *The past is important but only because it can help us make the present and the future fuller and more right.*

FIRST PETTING PARTIES

For the sake of feeling ourselves into the scenes we'll be considering, let's each of us imagine that we've just had a baby. Here we are, proud father or still-a-bit-woozy mother.

"It's a boy!" or "It's a girl!" (And here's one time, at least, when we can have whichever we want.) The hum of the hospital is buzzless, padded though bustling. Sterile, breathless and awesome! Don't touch. Don't breathe! "See, the pretty baby!" But you don't have any real chance to look.

A masked nurse carries it off, or holds it for a moment at a window for you to glance at—swaddled completely up to the chin and down past the feet. You want to ask, "Does it have toes? Ten of them? All healthy?" But you don't quite dare.

Then, if you're papa, you're told to "Come back in visiting hours! You have to get out of the hall now!" You notice the baby cart coming with a dozen or more white, cocoonlike packages yapping for food, and you wonder, bewildered, if any of these nameless bundles is yours. But you're pushed out unceremoniously and unsympathetically. No one seems to care about the ordeal you've been through. No one seems concerned that it's *your* baby they've snatched away from you when you want and need to know what it's like.

If you're mama, the story is even more defeating. "Are you sure he's all right?" . . . "Why, certainly, dear!" with off-hand, conciliatory dismissal resulting from long practice in room after room of anxiously demanding new mamas. "When can I see him?" . . . "Why, according to schedule, of course!"

According to schedule . . . according to schedule . . . according to schedule. . . .

That's all you hear or are supposed to think! But other thoughts do keep intruding, *I wish I could see him, get to know him, have him near me! I wonder if they pay enough attention to him?*

Perhaps you get courageous and venture, "Say, nurse, does he cry a lot?" . . . "Is he a good baby?" . . . or "Does he sleep well?" But you don't dare add the silly ones like, "Does he wrinkle his nose? Does he look cute when he yawns? What does he do all day long beside sleep?"

This sort of scene takes place in ninety-nine hospitals out of a hundred. But if you are fortunate, you are in that other *one* where the scene is miraculously different.

Your baby isn't tucked away in a nursery with impersonal anonymity. Your baby is in the room with you. And the theme song is changed from "In Praise of the Schedule" to a chorus of "Watching Your Baby," of observing what he's like and what he needs.

The arrangement they've made for you here is called "rooming in." More and more hospitals are adopting it, having seen that babies thrive on it better than on the impersonal mass care of the nursery. And curiously, more mothers have been able to nurse. Babies have sleep rhythms that vary. If a baby is brought to nurse when he's on one of his sleepy stretches, he fails to suck lustily. "He's naughty! too lazy." "He won't take the breast!" Actually, he is sleepy. But meanwhile, the mother's milk glands do not have the stimulation they need to carry on the nursing. "I wanted to nurse but I couldn't," you complain. But had your baby been with you, this complaint might have been offset.

By having your baby with you, you get to know him; you can find out with your own eyes and ears and fingertips what he is like. You can become familiar with his moods and his movements, with the funny little noises that he makes. You can get over feeling that he's a mysterious stranger. You can nurse him when he grows hungry and ready to nuzzle and suck vigorously. You can cuddle and love him and comfort him when he cries.

His father, too, will get to see him, possibly as the one and only privileged person allowed into the room. He, too, will become familiar with his baby's ways. Together the two of you will develop a sense of this baby's belonging to you both. And this will communicate itself to him.

By the time you go home you know about some of your baby's needs and wants. For one thing, you realize that cuddling doesn't hurt him. And this is the most fortunate thing that could happen. For *the free gift of love to your child in his first days is the best insurance against disciplinary casualties later*. It fills his greatest emotional need at this period in the best possible way. Picking up and cuddling a baby gives him a groundwork of basic security. It serves as foundation for his sense of belonging. It lets him know that he is wanted and tells him he is safe.

And yet, on all sides, you will hear challenges. "You don't mean that you pick up your baby at *any* moment he wants? Didn't you know you're supposed to stay on a schedule?" It seems you're supposed to confine love to certain specified times, like the husband and wife who set aside two regular

90

nights a week for love-making. As if love could be rationed and neatly scheduled instead of pouring itself out in the spontaneous, upsurging response with firm regard for another's needs and affectionate yearning to meet his wants.

The idea is ludicrous and a little abhorrent. But it represents exactly what has been done with many an infant. Instead of watching to see when he's awake, instead of following one's own hearty wish to have him close, instead of picking him up when he seems to want it, he's left to lie like a wooden papoose till the time rolls around and the schedule reads, "Now play with your child."

A mother speaks to her baby through body language. She tells him how she feels toward him through fondling him, through caressing him, through letting him nuzzle his face into her, through nursing him if she can when he shows he is hungry and through making up for not-nursing by many extra moments of holding him to her. She communicates to him through her body, through her warmth and her touch.

The baby in turn communicates in his way through wriggling, through restlessness, but, first and foremost, through raising his voice. Only he doesn't have words with which to communicate. He has only his cry.

When he is in need of us, he cries. When he is lonely or hungry or uncomfortable, when he is hurt or frightened, he cries. He cries to say, "Please come and rescue me." He cries to say, "Don't leave me here helpless, unhappy and lonesome." He cries to say, "I'm in pain."

If we are followers of the old way, we fail to heed him. We go about our business, frying a steak or reading a paper. We are convinced, come what may, that we are going to let him "cry it out." We mutter that we are not going to spoil him. And we fail altogether to realize that we *are* spoiling him, not figuratively, but in fact.

We are spoiling his disposition. We are spoiling his security.

91

We are spoiling his sense of belonging and safety. We are spoiling his happiness. And, not least in importance, we are spoiling his relationship with us.

What do we teach him as we disregard his attempts at communication? What do we show him about our devotion to him? Do we let him know that he can count on us for help when he needs us? Do we show him that we can be depended on to rescue him in his helplessness? Do we let him see beyond question that he can trust us to feel *with* him and to understand how he feels? Or does he find, in the earliest months of his life, that we desert him? That he actually can not count on us to hear or heed or understand? And that he himself is unable to achieve the communication of his wants?

Suppose for a moment that you were in his position. Suppose that you were confined to bed—say with a broken hip that kept you in one position as he is, unable to turn from one side to the other, unable to raise yourself or get up. Then suppose you were suddenly frightened or hungry or in pain and that you called out to ask for help. But lo, your husband or wife went on calmly about the business of reading the paper and frying the steak. . . . How would you feel? What would happen to your relationship? Obviously it would suffer. Obviously love would diminish and hurt and resentment would come in. This is certainly not what you would deliberately set out to do to your child. For, you realize by now, that it is just this sort of hurt and resentment that underlies later disciplinary ills.

We must stop thinking of a baby's cry as naughtiness. When he cries we should say to ourselves: "That is his way of talking. He's telling us that he needs us. By heeding his cry we satisfy his basic emotional hunger for love. We bring him a chance for achievement also on two scores because when we answer him, he can begin to feel, even though wordlessly: 'I *can* communicate my wants! And *I* myself can do something to help right conditions that are wrong!' " But, more important

92

even than these things, as we answer his call he discovers that he has parents who listen and hear and understand.

As we observe a baby with noticing eyes we see that he is no automaton to be left to lie like a lifeless doll. One father and mother saw this clearly for themselves. They were lucky people. They were aided in their observation by possessing one of the newly designed, air-conditioned cribs in which a baby can sleep and play without the encumbrance of clothes or covers. This Baby Haven looks like a small, one-decker bunk bed, or peasant wall bed with solid top and back and ends. The front is transparent, made of unbreakable plastic that slides easily open and shut. The air circulates continuously and with the scientific control of draft, temperature and humidity, the baby can lie without either clothes or bed covering. Through the thin walls and plastic panel his every sound can reach his parents' ears. "And you can really *see* him! He's not just a tiny head at the top of a bundle of covers. He's a *whole* baby . . . We've sat and watched him for long stretches. We were surprised to find how much he moved around even at three weeks, and we've been thrilled ever since to be able to see the increasing use he makes of his body and hands and his legs and feet."

Lacking this scientific crib, parents can learn a lot about a baby by giving him opportunities to play without clothes. But the child must be on a firmer and larger surface than the canvas table on which a few kicks a day too often suffice.

It's our right and our baby's right for us to play with him as well as for us to listen and to heed his cry. It's our right and his to enjoy life together. He'll cry much less and the question of disciplining him will become far less acute later if we cuddle him aplenty and play with him aplenty from the first moments of his life.

He likes to be picked up and held close. He likes to be patted on the back and stroked. He likes to be walked with. He likes the rhythmic movement of being rocked. He likes simple little songs and cooing noises and the old crooning body movements of mothers who have let themselves be natural and warm and spontaneous since the world was young.

BIBS AND BUCKETS

"When I'm hungry," says Bill, "I'm the crossest guy in the world!"

"I'm a bear!" answers Betty.

They laugh and decide that they'll get an ice-cream cone apiece. "There," with two contented sighs, "now we won't have to bite each other's heads off!"

But if you're a baby you have no recourse to ice-cream cones or to icebox maraudings. You're utterly and completely dependent on the big folk around you to come and rescue you from the hunger pangs in your tummy. Fortunately, these days all over the country parents are learning how important it is to feed their babies when they're hungry rather than when a certain time of the clock rolls around. Only the baby himself knows when this is! No one else can feel the pain in his middle when the hunger contractions begin. All we know is that the time between hunger contractions varies from infant to infant and varies in the same infant from time to time. After one feeding a baby may grow hungry within the hour; after the next feeding he may go for five hours; after the next, for two. Probably within the first few months of his life, he'll gradually regulate himself so that he's on a fairly even schedule, though babies differ in this respect too. But meanwhile, we will have listened and heeded his pleas to save him from hunger. We will have answered him when he called to us with the only means at his command—his cry. In this fashion we will have shown him that we love him and understand what he feels. NOTHING is more important! This we already know. For, when a child lacks love and understanding, the resulting hurt and fear and anger can produce disciplinary problems that may be difficult to clear.

Too often we make a fetish of routine. This is true not only with infants but with adults. We must eat at certain times, in certain positions and places. We must eat certain things at certain temperatures, cooked to a certain texture or consistency and combined with certain other foods or seasonings to give a certain traditional taste. We must eat with certain implements, holding them in certain traditional ways.

But obviously all of this can become very tedious. So why not explore how variations may come in?

For example: Wouldn't you yourself like a change from supper on the straight chairs at the dining-room table to eating in front of the fire, lolling lazily on the couch? How about dinner from a tray in the garden while you prop yourself on one elbow in the grass?

How about cold fish for you instead of hot? Or cold potato soup with a green splash of chives on top in the French manner? How about mashed peas fixed like mashed potatoes just for the change of consistency on your tongue? Or soft ice cream, runny as creamy custard? How about a little Mexican *cumino* on your eggs or Italian rosemary over your carrots? Or cottage cheese and spinach mixed with mayonnaise and molded into a salad?

As for staying politely with those timeworn instruments? Don't you yourself welcome holding chicken bones or spare ribs heartily in your hands? Or sucking the juice out of an orange? Cool chocolate through a straw? Hot coffee with a dash of brandy from a tall glass?

After all, it is fun to experiment and to find out which foods and flavors are most enjoyable.

It's fun to experiment with your child's feeding too and to find out what sort of things are most enjoyable for him. But first you have to divorce yourself from the do or-die attitude of unyielding routines and prescriptions and enter into mutual and shared exploration.

Some babies prefer to drink their orange juice or water or

milk while they're held in their mother or father's arms; some seem to prefer lying in their cribs. When they're fed, some like to lie propped up by a pillow; some like to sit up in a high chair before they are six months old and may then, after a few more months, want to go back to a lap position. Later on, some may even prefer to eat standing up!

Some like it hot; some like it cold! Some wrinkle their noses at warm milk and relish it fresh off the ice. Some like soft lumpy bits and virtually smack their lips over these, while others refuse food vigorously if it contains any suspicion of a lump . . . Incidentally, when he is first given solids, if his little tongue sticks out and his lips close and the food oozes all over, the baby is not deliberately spitting out his food in naughtiness. His muscular apparatus isn't ready yet. He isn't quite able to effect the coordinations needed to take in and swallow solid foods. So instead of forcing, we do best to wait a few weeks and then try again.

Some babies take a while to get used to solids and need to start very gradually on these. Some like solid food at their evening meal and dislike it in the morning. Some like beef scraped and some like it in chunks. Some like their cereal runny; some like it thick. Some like liver and peas and custard all mixed together; and some like each one distinct and alone . . . At times a child may go on a pea jag; at times he may want nothing but cereal and apple sauce for days at a time. It doesn't matter. In the end, it's been found by scientific observation, a child manages to even up the likes and dislikes so that a well-balanced diet results.

As for the timeworn business of implements and the tradition of manners: They mean less than nothing to a baby for quite some time. Dabbling in food and stuffing it in with fingers is far more enjoyable than using a hard, metal spoon.

In weaning, some babies make direct transition from breast to cup any time between seven and nine months; some who have been on the bottle need it on and on until long past the

96

time they are walking around. Some go back to the bottle for short periods after they have been successfully weaned. Usually this going-back occurs during an upset. Some children eat better and enjoy their food more if they have something to play with while they are eating. A spoon to bang or a milk bottle top to handle may prove a help rather than a hindrance. And, as for the mannerliness of eating in uninterrupted fashion, it just isn't done. As early as five months a baby may interrupt his feeding, look around, play, laugh and return to his food voraciously. In like manner, the two-year-old may jump up from the table, wander about the room and then joyously get back to devouring his meal.

As for quantities: We all know that appetite varies at different times. Nothing short of a huge steak will prove satisfying at times to our adult palates, while at other times a salad may suffice. A baby at one time may want only an ounce or two of a bottle, while at other times he greedily gulps down the whole. A child may nibble a crust of bread and want nothing more at one meal and scrape up the last of a heaping plate at the next.

It's far better to take all these likes and dislikes into consideration than to use up time and energy and tempers in forcing and fights. If we can relax and explore and discover what is comfortable and enjoyable to a child while he's little, we'll find that he fits in with the approved modes and manners far more readily later on.

The small child's life is so taken up with food and drink and the acts of his body that making his own choices in connection with these things constitutes important sources of achievement for him at this stage. If we go counter to what he decides and wants, we tell him that his choices are no good, that what he achieves isn't right. We create hurt and anger. And the anger gets into his eating and gets all mixed up with his food. He knows, then, that by refusing food he successfully hits out at his parents. By spitting it out or rolling it around in his mouth, by finickiness or by vomiting he makes them worry and so gets even. By stuffing, by eating them out of house and home and developing into the fat boy he saddens their souls.

Good feeding habits, as well as good dispositions, are helped if parents can join in the spirit and laugh with small children as they dabble and mess and go on food jags of one sort or another. Fun, associated with eating, is much more important at this early age than finishing meals with the finest of manners and with perfect dispatch.

There's a certain restaurant in San Francisco on the water front which serves *cioppino*—a marvelous dish of soup and shell fish still in the shell. With pomp and ceremony the waiters bring on big bibs and huge finger bowls so that those who partake may pare off the shells, mess to their heart's content and clean up with ease.

So—while your children are little, why not play the *cioppino* game? Why not pull out the big bibs and buckets and make things as easy and pleasant as they can be?

ALL-DAY SUCKERS

As we've said, the baby himself is the only person in the world who feels his own internal discomfort and needs. If his tummy is empty he alone knows its pangs. He alone knows how much food he must have in order to feel satiated and content. By the same token, only he knows how much sucking he must have.

Babies the world over have a natural and primitive need to suck. Through their lips they satisfy hunger. Through their lips they get their first feel of intimacy with another human being, their first experience of love. Through their lips they receive a very fundamental kind of sensory satisfaction or bodily pleasure. No wonder at times they look as if their whole life were focused on their mouths.

A baby nuzzles around with his lips as if he were using

them to search and to feel out the world of people and things. Into his mouth goes the food. In go the toys. In go blankets, sheets, gowns, fists, and, most handy of all available things—his thumb.

Ordinarily, all this sucking business means, quite simply, that he has not yet had as much sucking as he needs. Perhaps his feeding periods have been too limited, either in frequency or length of time, to satisfy his natural sucking wants. Perhaps, for other reasons, he needs to suck more. We're not the judges. He's the only one who can tell. And tell us he does, quite directly and clearly, by going after that thumb of his, do or die.

What then? Shall we bring out thumb-guards, aluminum mits, elbow cuffs, bitter lotions, or that recent hideous device that fits the curve of the upper teeth, has rakelike prongs which protrude down into the mouth and close on the intruding thumb like a gopher trap, making the child withdraw it in pain! Shall we by any or all means try to take sucking away from him? What if we succeed? Then he'll go along with the need to suck unsatisfied within him. He will never have sucked it out, as it were.

We will have failed him. We will have hurt him by not understanding his need. We will have hurt him by preventing him from satisfying it. Perhaps he grows angry at us in consequence and afraid of what we'll do. Then he gets the feelings of hurt and fear and anger all mixed into the sucking.

As he grows, instead of still trying to suck, he may angrily bite his nails or he may try other perverse forms of bodily gratification. He may, for instance, pull out handfuls of hair or take to head-banging. Or he may start to lick the paint off his bed or the paper off the walls.

How, then, shall we treat it when he sucks his thumb?

The simplest cure is to let him suck to his heart's content. To let him have his fill. To suck it out. Ordinarily, he then stops of his own accord after he has sucked enough.

"But," you cry, "meanwhile how about his jaw? Won't his mouth have become misshapen and deformed?"

Some dentists and doctors still believe that thumb-sucking makes teeth grow crooked. Among children whose teeth need straightening, they see any number who have sucked their thumbs. But they do not see those who have sucked thumbs and whose teeth do not need straightening.

One scientifically minded dentist, however, decided to get to the root of the matter. He took a group of thumb-suckers and compared them with a group of nonthumb-suckers by making repeated casts of their mouths as they grew. What he found shed considerable light. As expected, the baby teeth of thumb-suckers were often pushed out of line. But this was not the complete picture. He watched longer and took casts again when the second teeth came in. And here he discovered that a curious thing had occurred. He found just about the same proportion of crooked-toothed youngsters among the nonthumb-suckers as among those who had sucked their thumbs. In the latter group their teeth had corrected themselves. There was one exception to this finding: if a child went on sucking his thumb after the second teeth came in, then the chances of his teeth remaining crooked increased.

We know now that the best cure for sucking is to get enough sucking. And so, if a child of ours wants to suck his thumb, let's lean back and smile at him with equanimity. Let's not take the matter so strenuously that we raise barriers between him and his needed satisfaction and also between him and ourselves.

If we can start out in the right way at the beginning of his life, it's fairly simple. We can let him have as much sucking as he wishes without complicating the whole affair. But what if we've already tried a million and one torturesome devices to keep him away from his thumb?

Then, if our child is still young enough, we may need to do much as Jennie's mother did after she learned that sucking it out was the best way. One evening she came across Jennie sitting on the couch eyeing her with three-year-old slyness. Whenever her mother looked away, Jennie's thumb would pop into her mouth. When her mother looked back, out it would come.

Finally, Jennie's mother went and sat down and took Jennie onto her lap. "See here, darling" she said, "I've been making a big mistake telling you not to suck that thumb. It's all right, dear, for you to do it. You can start right now, whenever you want. Mommie won't scold anymore."

Jennie shook her head. "Mommie will spank."

"No, dear. I know you're afraid, but mommie won't spank."

"Mommie will put on nasty business!"

"No, dear, not the nasty-tasting stuff either."

"Jennie can suck?"

"Yes, dear, you can suck all you want."

For a while, according to Jennie's mother, the mistrust continued. But gradually, Jennie grew less and less shy in her sucking maneuvers. To use her mother's words, "She went on an orgy of sucking. She followed me around, one hand holding her teddy bear, the other hand in her mouth. She sucked in the bathtub, in bed, in the car, walking on the street. It took a lot of inner fortitude on my part to keep my hands from yanking *her* hand out of her mouth or from at least telling her to stop. Soon, though, the sucking grew less until it disappeared in the daytime. At nap and at night, though, it went on until Jennie was five. And then, it stopped completely and altogether."

It has been found that when sucking goes on and on it may have grown from a natural means of gratifying the sucking need to a device for bringing comfort to a child. He may be soothing himself for the lack of some sort of emotional need which we will then have to try to discover and supply. Or he may carry his sucking on and on as a means of expressing anger against us for hurts he feels we have given him. In any

101

case, when sucking persists we'll do better if we take a flank approach to discover and deal with the need that he lacks.

It has been found, however, that when a child's thumb-sucking goes into his second year it usually persists quite normally through the third year as well. Sometimes a pacifier can take the place of a thumb, but not always. The thumb still seems best.

THE MESSIER, THE MERRIER

Cuddling times, feeding times, times of crying-it-out and sucking times are crucial times in the first year of life. These times contain the child's first experiences of having basic physical and emotional needs either satisfied or denied. In consequence, these times are tied up with earliest hurts and fears and anger. So, too, are the times connected with a child's toilet training.

We know from studies that many activities which seem simple to us as adults call for muscular coordinations so complicated that a young child is actually not able to accomplish them. It's easy for us to pick up a small object and drop it into a cup. There's nothing to it. But for most children under a year of age it's an impossibility. When a child sets out to do this, he must make his hand go where his eye directs. He must make fingers and thumb close over the object, lift his hand, move it to a position directly over the cup, releasing his grip and, at just the right moment, drop in the prize. This involves a whole set of complicated muscular contractions and relaxations. It calls not only for muscles that are sufficiently mature but also for a mind mature enough to comprehend what is asked. Unless mind and muscles are ready, a child is not able to achieve the task.

In similar fashion, going to the toilet involves a complicated set of muscular contractions and relaxations and a mind ready to comprehend what is expected. A child must, for one thing, recognize the urge. He must quickly associate where to go, judge how long it will take to get there and, meanwhile, keep the muscles around his anus or urethra contracted until he achieves just the right position and just the right moment to let go and drop in the prize.

We know that those muscles on which his bowel control depends ordinarily become mature enough around ten months; that those on which urination depends can be counted on for some degree of control around the second birthday, but not for complete control until a child is about four. Ordinarily, he himself gives us certain signs that he is ready to learn urinary control. When he wakes up dry from his nap between eighteen months and two years and when he becomes interested in puddles and in water play, then we can say, "Now we can give it a try."

If we ignore his maturity levels and demand too early control we ask a child to accomplish the impossible. His muscles are not ready; much less his mind. He may not understand; he may have no real motivation to become trained until he's well along in his second year. If he is one of those "regular" children, we may be able to anticipate and catch him. But then the achievement of control is ours, not *his*, and sooner or later he resents this. On the other hand, if he is one of those "irregular" individuals, we start battling and anger right then. In either case, we are apt to create disciplinary problems where they would not need to be. And so, he fails in the achievement we expect.

Along with all this business of training, another sort of feeling has entered. Long before a child begins to learn control, he has found that eliminating is pleasurable. He has not yet built up our adult taboos about bowel movements and urination being messy or dirty. He frankly enjoys the relief from internal pressure. He also enjoys the sensory stimulation of the delicate nerve endings around the urethral and anal openings. And, in his hedonistic, baby way, he also enjoys against his body the warmth and softness of what he has

103

produced. He wants to keep these enjoyments; he does not want to give them up.

But he must gradually fit in with the patterns of cleanliness and control that our culture demands. A part of him wants to do this too. He wants our love. He wants to accomplish what we ask.

When a child has been loved and cuddled a lot and is happy and secure and then is trained gradually and slowly all in due time, he feels good about the thing. He feels big and important. He feels full of a sense of achievement and proud to do out of love for us what he can. "Here, honey," says three-year-old Tim, "here's a great big b.m. all for you!" To him this is a present he has produced for his mother. He has made it for her with his body. He looks on it as something of value that he himself has achieved.

To complicate the matter, however, the grownup may step in with scoldings and admonitions and with an enormous lot of feeling centered on cleanliness and success. Then the child begins to see that he disappoints and hurts his parents with his wetting or soiling or whenever his toileting does not move according to their dictates. But so, too, are they hurting him.

They are belittling him and making him feel that what was clean is dirty. That his body is dirty. That what he produces is disgusting. By their very tone of voice they do this. And sometimes they do it by additional affronts. If they use enemas or suppositories as part of the training program to induce movements at certain times, they add these to the previous list of indignities. To him, they are forcibly taking something away from him by intrusion into his body. This frightens him and makes his anger grow apace.

Inadvertently, too, they may also stimulate the sensory nerve endings which give him pleasure around his anus. They then induce him to mix up bodily pleasure with anger responses. Obviously, this may lead into all kinds of strange

104

quirks about the body and the dignity of the normal and natural pleasures it should have.

Suppositories or no suppositories, if elimination is made to seem wrong or unclean by parental emphasis, this not only hurts him. It makes him grow angry at his parents and afraid of them and afraid of himself too. He becomes afraid of what his body may do to get him in wrong. Later, perhaps, he ties this in with sex since the same region of his body is involved. In any case, he again gets hurt and fear and anger all mixed up with a natural process—this time with elimination. Then, in contrast to Tim's attitude of proudly bringing a gift to his mother, a child adopts a very different attitude toward what he produces. This is what four-year-old Ellen does.

"It's poison," she says. "I'll smear you with it!" She looks on her movement as a dirty, nasty thing and uses it as a kind of weapon with which to express anger. So, too, does John who, at ten, still exasperates and worries his mother with constipation that has persisted from the time he was very young.

Many children who soil or wet beyond the time when they should be clean are doing this out of anger against parents who trained them too young or too harshly or who denied them some or another fundamental satisfaction in the very early days of their lives. Says Blaine, eight, with a bright look of sadistic enjoyment, "I wet my bed every night. Then my mother cleans up with one hand and holds her nose with the other. Or she makes me do the clean-up job, but she still gets red and upset." Either way, through wetting Blaine has let his anger out.

Whether or not a child looks on the products of his body as clean or dirty, whether he takes them as a gift or a weapon, his interest in them will run high all through the early years. Nor is this surprising since, besides his natural interest, we have helped him focus on them by the emphasis we ourselves have placed on them.

We'll want, of course, to keep him feeling that his body

and its products are clean and wholesome. We'll want to prevent their getting mixed up with his anger and resentments. And so we'll try at least not to grow disgusted when he frankly enjoys what he does. If he sniffs contentedly at what he has done or examines it admiringly, if he has "accidents," even if he smears himself or his bed, we'll try to remember that his child feelings are not yet as "refined" as our own. We'll try to accept them and we'll try, also, to help him work them out. For we don't want them to stay in him and keep him in the grip of baby urges all his life.

Fortunately, as he grows we can, as with other feelings, help him channel these into activities which we can more readily condone. In fact, he himself will often do this spontaneously if we wait and give him the chance.

We'll notice, as we watch him, that his interest will wander from puddles in the bed and on the floor to puddles on the sidewalk and in the garden. His messing interest will divert itself to messing in mud and suds and paste and paint. He'll adore running the water in wash basins and tubs and watching it swish around in the toilet.

Ann is two and her mother has left a bowl of freshly mixed dough in the kitchen and has gone to answer the phone. When she comes back there is Ann sitting sedately on a chair, the most blissful look on her face. "What are you doing, honey?" Ann's mother asks. And then she sees. Ann has lifted the bowl onto the floor. She now wriggles her toes in the dough, obviously ecstatic. "It's gooey, all guishy, all doo-doo goosh!"

Recounting the story, Ann's mother says, "A short time back I would have raised my hands and shrieked. But I managed to keep calm. After all, twenty years from now I'll have forgotten the wasted minutes and eggs and milk and flour, but Ann might still have carried the scars of my disgust. So I said, mirroring her feelings, 'It feels good!' That was all I could manage for the time.

" 'Uh-huh,' she nodded, and again went into her song and dance. 'It's doo-doo guishy goosh!'

" 'Come on, baby,' I said, 'I'll get you some better doo-doo goosh; that's mommy's there!' And I took her outside and we dug and poured and made a mudhole and got her undressed and let her wallow. The next morning I made some starch paste for rainy days so she could get out the doo-doo gooshing to her heart's content. And she did."

Tolerating a child's interest in the products of his body, letting his enjoyment of them channel out through various wet and "gooshy" activities * and, best of all, enjoying such activities with him may help him pass through the baby phase with healthy attitudes toward elimination. It can also help him in his lifelong attitudes toward himself and his body and can keep away a lot of troubles, including disciplinary ones.

THE INSISTENT I AND THE CONSTANT NO

Many infants pass through the first baby stages with very little need for discipline. They are the "regulars." They eat regularly, evacuate regularly, sleep regularly. Usually there's a reason for this even though we aren't aware of it. Their natural rhythms fit into the required rhythms so that few clashes of their will against their parents' come into focus. In contrast, the "irregulars" may clash continuously. Their own rhythms of eating, of eliminating, of sleeping either do not fit the prescribed intervals or have no fixed pattern but vary from day to day or week to week.

Comes a day, however, when both regulars and irregulars develop an exaggerated mind of their own. Especially with the regulars does it seem exaggerated in contrast with what has gone before. They are no longer content to be dropped into their cribs or playpens. They no longer are as willing to remain compliantly quiet and out of the way.

Around the end of the first year or on into the second,

* See Chapter 12 for many more activities of this sort.

107

children grow eager to explore, to assert themselves, to feel their oats, as it were. They want what they want when they want it. They are insistent little egoists. Every urge must have an immediate answer. No pleasure must be deferred.

They wander around, grabbing objects, pulling out plugs, pulling down vases, sticking ash trays in their mouths, emptying cigarettes all over the floor.

"No, no!" says mother repeatedly. But her child's only answer lies in competently ignoring her and completely centering on himself, his impulses, his wants.

"No, NO!" she persists, quite a bit louder; adding, with a swift rap at his knuckles, "Don't you touch!"

But he must touch. He must find out about the world which surrounds him. This is his way of discovering the world. He must get the feel of it through his fingers and lips, through his toes and his nose as well as through his eyes and his ears. This is one of his first adventures in independence, in finding himself as an entity in the world.

Swiftly another adventure follows. He must try himself out. He must test his ability to stand on his own even though he still stands in a wobbly way. He must assert himself further in order to gain concrete confirmation that he does have a self to assert. And so, he shakes his head when mother shakes hers and he answers her "no" with a well-rounded "no" of his own.

Everything's "No!"

"Come here!"

"No."

"Want your dinner?"

"No."

"Put the glass down!"

"No."

Or his eyes twinkle and he regards his mother with calm disregard.

During the second year of his life, all this mounts and grows worse. The no's become more constant. They seem to pervade every scene.

This is still a child's way of testing out himself and his strength. It is his way of seeking to achieve the beginnings of independence. It is his way of saying, "I want more of ME" rather than "I want less of YOU." At least at the start. The emphasis is on finding himself rather than on losing us.

For he still wants and needs a lot of us. We see this continuously in the dependence and clinging that still characterize his behavior. At one moment he is the big self-asserter wandering around the yard, pulling the pansies, scattering the trash. And then, suddenly when a friendly stranger passes and says, "Hello, baby!" he reddens, yelps and flees into our sheltering arms. His independence is very tenuous. His dependence is far deeper and far more real.

We can make his uncertain independence gain a spurious semblance of certainty if we handle it unwisely.

If our child has one of those rugged characters, our efforts to stop the explorations and down the no's only increases them. He doesn't feel strong underneath, but he's hurt at our interference with his achievement and he's angry as a result. So, he stubbornly pursues his wanderings and works in as many no's in the course of the day and night as he possibly can, not only to cover his hurt and to give himself at least a self-protective semblance of strength, but also to hit out at us and to annoy us all he can. On the other hand, if our child has one of those meek personalities, he chooses more roundabout ways of protecting himself and of getting even. Possibly instead of saying so many no's in a downright open way, he now lets the no out by refusing food or refusing to sleep. Possibly he annoys us by clinging all the more to a bottle or to a thumb.

In any case, our fighting calls forth his fighting and intensifies his negative bent. And so a child may turn into the

109

rebellious adolescent or the husband who refuses to pet his wife or the wife who perversely serves her husband food he doesn't like. For many times the negative attitude in adolescence and adulthood is simply a carry over from earlier days when the no's were *fought* and *fortified.*

An excessively negative attitude in the second and third year of life may result from a too-active fighting of the child's no's by the adults. Or it may come from lacks in meeting his cuddling or feeding needs or what not in his first years.

No matter which, wiser handling of the child's initial attempts at independence can do a lot.

Instead of forbidding him to handle and feel out objects in the world about him, we do better to place within his reach things that he can freely explore. We can put the cigarette boxes and the flower vases on top of the mantel at least while he's around and arrange sturdy, unbreakable ornaments on low places or replace these with things that can stimulate his learning and make his discoveries worth while. Some pans that fit into each other or a set of well-washed ash trays of graded size can well replace china bowls or delicate statuettes. A sturdy wooden box with a block inside or a few stones from the garden can well replace the box of cigarettes. Then our child can, as example, manipulate and experiment to his heart's content, shake the box, listen to the sound, open it, take out the stones, touch the surface with his lips and tongue and fingers.

Later, when he discovers the electric plug or floor heater, we can play "touch" and "discovery" games with him. "The plug feels smooth, not rough like the garden rocks." The prongs "stick out." The surface is "hard, not soft like the pillow on the couch." "The plug goes *in*—this way. See how mommie does? You do it with me if you like."

Instead of meeting resistance with resistance, instead of countering no with no, we do better to go back to our old rules of mirroring and accepting what the child is feeling
110

behind his words. . . . "You don't want to do what mommie says. You want to do what you want. Yes, I know," with a nod and a smile and an awareness of the meaning of all this to him. Then, in a few moments, if the thing to be done is important, we can follow up by rephrasing what we've asked. We'll find frequently that the rephrased request is blithely acceded to when it follows on the heels of our acceptance and our mirroring of the negative no.

"It's bedtime, Tommy."

"No. No. No."

"You don't want to come."

"No!" angrily. "Bed's naughty. Naughty daddy."

"You don't like daddy because he thought of taking you to bed."

So you wait a few minutes and then say pleasantly, "Okay now. Ready for bed!" And Tommy reaches out his arms and echoes, "Okay."

When a child is in the negative period, it's especially important to cut down as many requests and requirements as we possibly can. There are so many biological rules which limit his behavior and curtail his independence that piling a lot of extra rules on him only intensifies his unrest and his sense of defeat. The ineptness and unreadiness of his muscles alone prevent him from much independent functioning. He wants to catch a ball the way big brother does. But he can't catch. He wants to turn on the electric light. But he can't reach. He wants to unwrap a package of orange drops but his fingers can't manipulate the tight paper. And so it goes. The load of really *necessary* restrictions in early childhood is so enormous that we should cut down on every possible unimportant, artificial, unnecessary thing. Many modes and manners will come later, naturally and easily. Our task is not to issue more rules but to reduce them now.

Actually, there are only a few rules that are essential to health and safety. Staying off the street. Not playing with fire. Not turning on the gas. Not grabbing a hammer to smash things when he gets angry. These are among them. But arranging physical barriers, like fences and safety valves and out-of-reach places for hammers and matches, can be more effective and less wearing than arguments and admonitions on and on.

We know now that a small child, if he is not harassed and worried and resentful, will eat and sleep and carry out the things that are necessary for his physical well-being quite of his own accord. We know now, for instance, that we don't even need to insist on so and so many hours of rest; that, left to himself and given the chance to rest, a child makes up for any losses of sleep quite of his own accord. Different children need different amounts of sleep anyway. Children, on the whole, move naturally in their sleep twice as much as adults. They take almost twice as long naturally to become quiet and go to sleep. Their sleep hours vary from night to night and from day to day. But unless we make sleep a fighting matter, in the course of any given two- or three-week periods they will have caught up with themselves and their own sleep needs.

When a child keeps calling for this and that, when he shows that he does not want us to leave him, our wisest procedure is to avoid fighting. The more he fights, the less like sleep will he feel. We do best if we put him quietly in bed and sit down quietly beside him, planning to avoid all rush and fuss. "You don't feel like going to sleep," reflecting, goes much further than a comamnding "Go to sleep now." . . . "You want mother to stay with you" goes further than an adamant "I won't stay!"

If our purpose is to get him to sleep—then this is our best policy. If our purpose is to win the fight against him, then of course it's a different matter.

As long as we're pulling *with* him for *his* best interests, our aim will be to keep our focus on the way he is feeling. It's better to work *with* him for a few weeks than to pull against

112

him so that anger may become more important to him than sleep. After all, the knowledge that he is understood and accepted is more conducive to sleep than being scolded and fought. In terms of over-all policy again, the soundest adage is to reduce the restrictions and enforcements and to follow the small child in his own rhythm of life.

HARDENING HIM TO MEET HARDSHIPS

"But if you let him do everything he wants when he's little, won't he expect to go on doing and having everything he wants as he grows? He has to meet frustrations. The world doesn't treat him with constant kindness," we may protest. "He has to learn to withstand hardships. Why not train him to do so when he is young?"

It may not sound correct but it is nonetheless a fact that children harden more readily and more firmly when they are not hardened too fast. Too many hurts or hardships *at any age* can break a person. This we know. Many a man committed suicide during the depression years, unable to stand the weight of difficulties. Many of us have felt ourselves on the verge of going over a precipice when the exigencies of life grew too great. Studies have shown that animals, sheep and cats and rats, break when frustrations grow too heavy.

A small child is neither an animal nor an adult. He is powerless in so many ways. He lacks the adult's background of knowledge and his ability to reason why things happen. He lacks the muscular coordinations that might carry him through in the canny fashion that an animal's body does or in the more mature fashion of the human adult.

When he is little, he has to endure a great many frustrations. As indicated earlier, a load of these comes as a result of biological restrictions alone. Another load comes as a result of large and important cultural restrictions. A baby wants to change his position to ease his body. He can't when he is tiny. He wants to run as fast as the bigger boys. The immaturity of his muscles holds him back. He wants to reach up and take a toy down from the mantel to play with. He isn't tall enough. His feet won't carry him fast enough and steadily enough to grant him many sorts of achievement he craves; his arms aren't long enough; his hands aren't adroit enough.

When he is small he would like his mother all to himself. He cannot have her. His father is there and other children. He cannot get rid of the younger brother or sister who comes to plague his life further. He cannot remain the cherished baby, much as he would like to. Nor can he escape the inevitable illnesses and physical discomforts that come into every child's life to defeat the primitive impulse for bodily comfort and ease.

These are large and inescapable frustrations. Just because he is little, he cannot comprehend why such things should be. The load may become heavy indeed.

Why, then, should we make the load heavier by adding an artificial burden? We know now that a child is better able to handle frustrations if the load is not too large when he is small. We know that hurt and fear and anger enter when frustrations have to do with basic needs. We know that disciplinary problems then increase.

The thing that makes a child best able to withstand life's hardships is an early sense of security. An early sense of safety. A feeling that he has firm ground beneath him on which to sally forth.

This comes through his feeling loved and accepted. Of paramount importance is his sense of confidence in us. *We* are his security. *We* are his world.

As we are harsh, his world is harsh. As we are cruel, his world is cruel. As we take his sense of confidence away from him, he loses confidence in everything and everyone including himself. He becomes weak, not strong.

In short, he learns best to meet hardships as the sense of his own strength grows. Too many hardships, coming too early, break his strength and his confidence. They make him cringing and unable to meet the inevitable difficulties that every life contains.

The hardening process lies in another direction: that of early satisfactions freely given by parents who consistently let him know he is loved.

"Don't say it, Mom. No matter what it is, I won't do it!"

IF HE NEEDS TO BE A BABY AFTER HE'S NO LONGER A BABY

Suppose he hasn't had enough cuddling. Suppose he's been left to cry it out. Suppose his sucking has been curtailed. Suppose his toilet training has been of the very worst sort. Suppose that his no's have been fought until his achievement of independence has been sadly damaged. Suppose, from all these early things, he has piled up hurts and fear and anger. Shall we hang our heads in shame? Berate ourselves? Tell ourselves mournfully or defensively, "It's too late now"?

115

No indeed.

The hurts are there, yes. But we can often make up for them. For, as we observe a child closely, we'll see that he often goes back to baby days and ways as if he himself were automatically seeking to make up for missed values or to work out the baby parts.

The child who sleeps irregularly, who does not want to go to bed, who jumps up a dozen times a night may belatedly be protesting the overregularity that curtailed feeding satisfactions for him earlier. Or he may be trying to make up for the no's that he could not say straight out in his baby years.

The child who steals may be clutching at values that failed to come to him through cuddling as an infant, and he may at one and the same time be hitting out in anger for having been denied the affection he needed. The child who never hears may be disguising his baby no's by not heeding now.

Although the ramifications are numberless, the ways of treating them can be summed up fortunately into a few, and by now familiar, steps. There are two big facets to these:

SUPPLY THE WANTS even
though belatedly.
PROVIDE OUTLETS for the
feelings of hurt or anger
or fear.

William, ten, was one of those perpetual whiners. His father had nicknamed him the "Whimper-will." "Cut it out, William—" in disgust—"you sound like a baby."

Came a day, however, when William's father and mother sat down together and began to take stock. "He does sound like a baby. Perhaps he's after some of the baby nourishment he failed to get. We were idiots not to cuddle him, but we didn't. That's obviously one of the things he wants—more love. But, quite obviously, we're not going to take him and rock him like a baby—the great big whopper! But we can love him in other ways a lot more than we do. Let's try an arm about the shoulder every so often and a loving pat on the back, a bear hug every once in a while when he wants one and the kind of looks and smiles that are cozy and warm.

"That ought to help supply at least one of the satisfactions he lacked!"

"Yes. But we'll also have to go further. We know from a lot of things he does that he's still holding grudges against us for the lack of love he felt in the past. Perhaps his whining is at least in part the anger coming out in a disguised form. So we ought to give him better chances to get it off his chest . . ."

Came William, whining. "I don't like milk! I don't want custard!" . . . "Why do I have to go to bed?" . . . "Oh gee, Pop, can't you take me to the show?"

"Look here, kid. I know you feel mean and unhappy and want to scold us right and left. We haven't been too good as parents. We haven't done a lot of things as we ought. We started wrong when you were a baby and now everything seems wrong to you. Better let us have some of the gripes straight off the chest!"

William voiced them, then, a whole long line, from not liking to get up in the morning to not liking to go to bed at night. But, as he went on and on day after day on a regular griping orgy, his parents noticed that one thing had happened. The baby whine had gone from his voice.

"Did you hear?" asked his father triumphantly later. "He was griping straight out like a man."

This at least was one step forward. Others came gradually as William's parents continued to help him get the baby parts out.

Sometimes a baby need for cuddling can later be made up for by extra chunks of love in whatever form fits the child's stage of development. Sometimes a baby's need to have us heed his cry of communication can be made up for by extra

117

attention to whatever communication he now attempts. Baby fears and hurts and anger can often be gotten out at a later stage of life. More suggestions will come as we read on. Meanwhile, a big part of our job is to know: It's never too late!

8. The hopeless rival

In our culture we have greatly idealized the picture of what family life should be. All peace and harmony. No rattling of the little bones of contention. No rivalry. No pushing or jostling of any one member by another in an attempt to gain first place. The sentiments of Isaac Watts have carried over from the eighteenth century and are still current in the twentieth. We still contend that

> Birds in their little nests agree;
> And 'tis a shameful sight
> When children of one family
> Fall out, and chide, and fight.

What is considered even worse is for children to chide or fall out or fight with their fathers or mothers.

And yet, as we have seen, human beings are human. They have nasty as well as nice feelings, hateful as well as loving ones. They have hurts and fears and angry feelings. And not infrequently these are augmented by the necessity to appear to get along happily together without ever daring to let rivalry or resentment show.

It's quite natural for a smaller child to feel inferior and to resent an older one. It's quite natural for an older child to be fearful of losing his special place when a newcomer arrives, and it's just as natural to feel hostile as a result. It's quite normal for children to vie with each other for mother's and

119

father's attention. It's normal even for them to vie with father for mother's attention or with mother for father's. When we make a child even unconsciously deny these normal feelings, we only produce in him a feeling of guilt so that he may cry in anguish as did thirteen-year-old Noreen, "I'm a terrible person. I'm not nice. Sometimes I think I'm crazy, I

Junior: "It's no fun growing old."

get such frightful feelings. I hate my brother and then wish I were dead. I'm not worth living and he is; he's so much better than I am. They all say he is."

Any adult who professes to love a husband or wife or child *all the time* is really either not being honest with us or with himself. Any child who avers that he loves his father and mother or sisters and brothers all the time isn't being honest either. He is disguising his real feelings. And this is not good. It only makes our problems with him increase. A far healthier way is for him to bring out his feelings and face them and

120

work them off. Then hostility can diminish and lovingness can increase.

THAT LITTLE RED BABY

Says the mother of several children, "You think you've got disciplinary problems with one child. But just wait till you have another. Then your troubles really start."

"Oh no," says the mother of one and two-thirds children, "Molly's going to adore having a baby brother or sister. She can hardly wait."

To Molly, "It'll be so nice, honey, having a darling little sister or brother."— "It'll be *your* baby. You can help me dress and bathe it."

From three-year-old Molly, "Will it splash in the tub?"

Absent-mindedly from mother, "I guess so." And with enthusiastic return to salesmanship, "You'll be so glad, Molly. You'll have someone to play with right in our own house. You won't be lonesome anymore."

At last the day arrives when mother and baby return from the hospital. Molly views the newcomer with a long and silent stare. And then, with very evident disgust, she accosts her mother, saying, "He can't play with me. Why did you make him so small?"

We've learned that preparing a child for the advent of a baby is important. Many of us do this well as far as we go. The only trouble is that we don't go far enough. We let the child share in the arrangement of room and clothing for the baby. We wisely communicate the "facts of life." We tell him in advance that mother will go to the hospital and will be back in a few days. We are careful to have him get acquainted in advance with the person who is to take care of him while mother is away if he does not already know and like this person.

But almost invariably we err in one very important part of the preparation. We paint a picture of sunshine and roses

121

and leave out the rain clouds and thorns. We forget two things: First, we forget that a baby inevitably has moments in which he becomes somewhat of a burden to everyone in the house. We neglect to say as part of the preparation, "Sometimes the baby will cry and worry us—maybe in the middle of the night. Maybe he'll wake us up and we won't like that. Sometimes you won't like it either when you feel that mommy or daddy give him too much attention. Sometimes you'll feel that he's a nuisance and a pest. . . . Sometimes you'll love him a whole lot; sometimes you won't like him at all."

Second, we forget that resentment will fly in *our* direction as well as at the new baby. For frequently a child grows angrier at his mother as the attention-giver than at the baby as the attention-getter. He may not show this, however, for it's safer and not quite so bad to be angry at the baby. Meanwhile, he keeps many of his angry feelings inside and they frighten and hurt him and do him untold harm.

And so, as part of our preparation, we need also to say, "Sometimes you'll be mad at mommie too. You'll want to tell her, 'Stop loving that little red baby. Come and love me.' Of course mommie will give you more loving whenever you want it. So, be sure to ask."

Ned's mother included all this in preparing Ned. "Sometimes you won't like the new baby," she said, when she was seven months along.

"I don't like him already!" announced seven-year-old Ned with direct and charming honesty.

"Tell me about it."

"Well, you people make such a fuss about him as if you'd never had a baby before. And he's not even here. When he comes it'll be a double mess for everybody."

"You feel it will be a mess for you."

"You bet I do. I might as well move out right now."

"You feel angry at us for making so much fuss over the new baby. And you think we're neglecting you."

122

"Yep!" In a few moments, however, Ned turned thoughtful. "Say, Ma, did you ever make such a fuss over me?"

"We surely did. And you want us to still, don't you?"

"Because all you do is to think of that thing in your stomach."

"I know how you feel, dear. Come on over and I'll give you a hug and we'll see if that doesn't help."

"But why," you ask, "shall we put these negative ideas into a child's mind?"

Why? Because he's bound to have such ideas after the baby's arrival no matter how carefully we try to prevent them. He's bound to have moments of anger at him and anger at us. And we'll want him to come to us with these ideas rather than suffer through them by himself. Otherwise, he and the new baby may never get to love each other with a wholesome and rugged kind of child-to-child loving. They will run too great a risk of their affection for each other never developing beyond a coat of glossy veneer which leaves their real feelings hidden but ready nonetheless to spring out in one or another disguise.

Eighteen-year-old Margaret, looking back, suddenly realizes that she had been living out just such a disguise. "I always thought I adored my younger sister," she said. "She's a darling! So sweet and pretty and onto herself. I've been shy and awkward in comparison, though my mother tells me I wasn't that way until I was six." She paused, looking puzzled. "Why, that's when my sister was born! Isn't that funny? I never thought of it before! Could I have been jealous? I never thought I was. I'd give my sister the shirt off my back or anything I had. Even chewing gum, and that was my favorite thing in life. I had a habit of breaking off a little piece from the wad I was chewing and popping it into her mouth. I knew she shouldn't swallow it, but it didn't ever hurt her. So, without anybody discovering it, I went right on doing it. I loved to see her chew and smack her lips. One day, though, I remember I gave her too much. So I put my hand down her throat to get it back. *I could have killed her! . . .*"

All at once Margaret stopped. "What am I saying? I could have killed her? I guess I could have. I guess, maybe, I wanted to. She was so cute and pretty, they all fussed so much over her, it hurt me a lot."

As Margaret went on, she realized clearly that she had been hurt by her sister's advent. She had felt a loss of parental love. As a result, she had grown angry and had wanted to get the baby out of the way. And so she had fed her gum and had tried to choke her. But she had been quite unaware of what her real motives were. She had managed for years to disguise her hostility. She had turned it against herself, annihilating herself with inferiority feelings instead of annihilating her sister.

When we make children ashamed of the jealousy and resentment, these feelings must come out in various disguises. One child coughed for months after the birth of a brother; another took out his aggression in cruelty to animals; still another in setting fires that might "burn the baby and his mother up." And yet, each one of these children was outwardly so devoted that his mother averred, "He isn't jealous. He adores the baby. I'm sure of that."

Once more we need to observe with open mind and sensitivity. When we notice that a child is jealous, we need to go back to the rules of accepting his feelings and of helping him get them out.

Terry and Sissy's parents did a good job of it once they learned. But that wasn't until Sissy was two and Terry four. By this time Terry was biting his nails badly and was tense and restless, a "veritable bundle of nerves." But they did not connect any of this with the baby until they took Terry to a psychologist.

"I know one thing," said Terry's mother in telling about Terry. "He hasn't an ounce of jealousy in him. He's the soul of devotion to Sissy. He insists on tucking her into bed every
124

night and he kisses her so sweetly. If she ever cries or is hurt, he gets awfully upset."

But in a play session in the psychologist's office some very different things came out. Terry was fascinated by dolls representing a family just like his own. He soon began to call the boy doll Terry and the girl doll Sissy. In short order, then, he took the Sissy doll and stuffed her into a toy toilet. "Go in there," he said. "I'll stick your feet in, you dumb biddy. I'll stick your hands in. I'll stick your neck and your nose in and I'll smear you all up and I'll drown you down the sewer."

Terry had been jealous. He was tense and "nervous" as a result of his continual effort to keep his real feelings in. The meaning of his nail biting and other facets of his behavior came out much later.

The program mapped out for Terry included sending him to a nursery school so that he might gain a sense of having certain rights and privileges which the baby could not yet have. Here a very sensitive teacher watched him closely. One day she saw him take an ordinary wooden block and call it "Sissy dolly." Then he fetched a bit of clay and deliberately smeared it over the block. Roughly he rubbed it around and around, chanting in a low voice,

> Cover dolly's
> Mouth with clay . . .
> She doesn't like it
> But—
> I have to do it.
> She's a bad, bad girl. . . .

As so often happens when a child starts to bring out his aggression directly, Terry went berserk for awhile. He wanted to push Sissy. He wanted to pummel her. But here his mother and father stepped in adroitly. This was a part of their job. They stopped his actions and yet at the same time they accepted his feelings. "We know you feel real mean to Sissy. But you can't hit her, dear."

125

And then they helped him steer his actions so that the feelings would flow into other channels, knowing how important it was for him to get the poison out.

They were by now well prepared for just these moments. They had bought Terry a rubber sister doll. "Let's see if you can't show us with this Sissy doll instead."

Terry complied for a while. And then one day he protested, saying, "But that's not the real Sissy."

"You want to do things to the real Sissy, but you can't, darling. You can do anything you want to this Sissy, though."

To this Terry brought a curious answer. "But you don't look!"

For a moment his mother was puzzled. And then the light dawned. When Terry annoyed the real baby, she *had* to focus on him. He succeeded in getting her away from Sissy. But if he pummeled the doll, she could quietly dismiss him from her thoughts. Terry had felt the difference. She would have to change this.

"You feel I won't pay attention to you if you're mean to Sissy doll, but I will. I want to see what you do. Show me, dear."

Terry sighed and attacked the doll half-heartedly. But as he found that his mother continued to focus on him, his resistance disappeared.

"You're a bad, bad baby!" He spanked and pinched and grew more and more violent. "Naughty baby. You make yourself wet. I got to spank you. . . ." And then, Terry did a very curious thing. His voice changed to one of sweetness. He kissed the baby doll. "I love you so much, honey. I have to eat you up." And he bit the doll as hard as he could.

This he continued for hours on end.

The meaning of the nail biting was clear at last. It had been a coverup for wanting to bite Sissy. But instead of biting her he had turned the biting onto himself. Other meanings were also apparent. His excessive concern with Sissy's getting injured and his excessive sweetness to her—these had not
126

been real expressions of love but rather disguises for the resentment he bore. The sweeter he was, the more he could cover the feelings of which he was ashamed.

Gradually, with the letting out of resentment, a more hearty, natural love for Sissy came into being. At times, Terry still scolded her; at times, he loved her. At times he treated

Mother: "We're going to have a dear little baby for you."
Sissy: "But, Mommie, I wish you'd have a pony instead."

her kindly, at times he teased and tried to hit. But there was nothing of the earlier forced and strained devotion that had been actually no devotion but pretense and sham.

Even with a very young child the same principles work all through. Linn was only eighteen months old when her sister came. For three months beforehand, Linn paid periodic visits to her grandmother so that this would not be a new and strange experience connected with the baby's birth. Beforehand, too, her mother told her quite simply, "We're going to have a baby." "Baby?" . . . "A little baby!" . . . "Little baby!" Her mother also made up a story which had to be repeated by request performance dozens of times. "Baby will sleep—like this!" [closing her eyes]. "Baby will yawn

127

like this! Baby will sneeze like this! And baby will cry yah, yah, yah!" [All this with suitable sounds and gestures.] "And sometimes Linn will say, 'Nice baby.' And sometimes Linn will say, 'Go 'way, baby, you're a nuisance; you take too much of my mommie's time!'" Always at this point Linn would laugh with relish.

After the baby came the story was continued with new embellishments to fit the occasion and with Linn's taking over the telling and adding bits of her own, varying from a pleased "Baby's sleeping!" to an exasperated "Naughty baby, cry!"

As has been brought out, a child is often more resentful to the mother than to the sister or brother. Four-year-old Josie, as example, was visibly upset after the birth of her baby brother. She went back to the baby way she had had of sucking her thumb.

One day Josie stood watching her mother nurse the baby. All of a sudden she reached out and pinched her mother hard.

"I know you're mad at me, darling, for holding the baby so close and feeding him and doing things for him all the time. I know you want to pinch me. But I can't let you do that. Here's this pillow, though. You can call it 'mommie' and you can hit or kick or pinch it instead."

Josie pinched and punched and kicked and hurled abuse at the pillow. "You're a bad mommie. I don't like you!" And then she added cannily, "I'll call the policeman and have him take the baby away from you. You're so bad you don't deserve him anymore."

As the days and months wore on and as Josie continued to get out her feelings of hostility to both the mother and brother, an easier and more peaceful relationship came. But during this time Josie's mother did not rely solely on Josie's getting the meanness out. She also planned her time carefully so as to give Josie an extra supply of the emotional values which Josie felt had been taken away by the new baby.

She arranged special times when the baby was sleeping in which she would play with Josie, shoving everything else aside.* She would take Josie on her lap and cuddle her, giving her big, extra doses of loving. During these moments an interesting thing happened. Josie began to play that she was the baby. She made little baby noises and rubbed her face against her mother's breast.

"You want a turn being my baby!"

Josie made more baby noises, snuggled closer, kicked her feet as the baby did, cried like the baby, laughed like the baby, too. "Now you pat me like the baby." So her mother did. "Now you burp me!" So, big as Josie was, her mother held her up against her shoulder and Josie went through the burping act.

But one day there came the prize demand. "Now feed me like the baby."

For a moment, her mother was nonplussed. Then, thinking quickly, she said, "I can't darling. You're too big. When brother gets a little bigger I won't nurse him either. I'll give him a bottle. Shall I show you how?"

She went and fetched a nursing bottle and put some milk in it. She took Josie up on her lap and held her close as if she were feeding a baby.

"Yum, yum," said Josie. "Baby thinks it's good." And slyly, "But not as good as eating mother up."

"You'd rather eat mother."

"Sure. But I can't."

Quite realistically, Josie had accepted the necessary limitations. She had met them quite contentedly since so many of her needs had been supplied and since so much of her resentment had been drained off. Incidentally, the thumb-sucking decreased as the contentment increased in Josie's life. No specific measures had been directed toward "curing" it. The more basic approach had worked far better.

* See Chapter 10.

Almost always, although children may not be as outspoken as Josie, an older child wants to take the baby's place. Perhaps he lets this wish out in disguised ways. He may go back to his baby days by wetting or soiling when he has long since been dry and clean. He may return, as Josie did, to sucking a thumb, a habit long since given up. Or he may come out directly, as she did later, and express what is on his mind.

We have passed the day when we condemn a child for letting us know his wants and needs. We are glad of the chance to know what to supply. We have passed the day when we berate a child for being courageous enough to bring the troubled feelings out directly. We're grateful when he does not resort to subversive, substitute, roundabout ways.

By saying "yes, dear," we accept and mirror his feelings. "I know how you're feeling. I used to feel the same kind of mean feelings sometimes. Everyone does."

By saying "yes, dear," we encourage him to get the poison out. "Tell me or show me more." And we watch and listen as he does. We don't turn our backs and go ahead with other business, because then we defeat our end. We only make him feel once more that we must disregard his "badness" instead of accepting it wholeheartedly as it spills.

We may have to curb actions that are harmful, hurtful or dangerous and provide substitute channels for feelings to flow through. "Look, dear, you can't hit the baby, but you can hit the rubber baby" . . . "You can't pinch me, but you can pinch that rag-doll mother over there!"

"I know, dear" is most important, for we must supply the lacking emotional nourishment, "I know you want more loving!" And you pick up your child and give him some good, warm hugs.

TOO BIG TO BEAT

It's not only the new baby who begets the jealousy in a family. There are many rivalries running in all sorts of cross-currents. Each child has his own special problems with every other child.

"I felt shunted off into the corner because I wasn't a boy like my brother, and boys were at a premium in our family. But I could never tell anyone how I felt. All I could do was to let it pile up inside until it made me so sick I'd vomit. I still get nauseated when the least little thing goes wrong."

"I was the fourth and the older ones were either better looking or cleverer. I always wished I were one of them. I've spent most of my life wishing things instead of getting out and doing them."

"I was the middle one of three with no rightful place of my own, or so it seemed. The older one got there by virtue of being bigger and better, the younger one because of being the baby. I was always in-between and still am. In every job I still step into the middle of something I don't want."

It's natural for children to have feelings against one another. The more they can work out such feelings while they are growing, the less will these perpetuate themselves as life goes on.

It's up to you NOT TO STOP THE RIVALRY FEELINGS or the meanness from coming out but to rechannel them when necessary by helping children CHOOSE HARMLESS RIVALRY ACTS.

If a child runs up tattling, and you're doing things in the old way, you'll say, "I don't want to hear that." But if it's the new way you're following, you'll listen and get his feelings and say them back. "You want to tell me. You're feeling real mean."

If your two youngsters are on a tear, quarreling and fighting and teasing each other, let's see what you do. Let's take the old you, first, doing things in the old way; the new you next, disciplining in the new way you're just learning.

Here are your two children, Micky and Jane. Jane is almost seven, Micky almost five. It's one of those pleasant afternoons when everything happens. The pilot on the stove wouldn't light. The telephone kept ringing. The grocery boy brought

131

the order all wrong. And then, Jane's new rabbit got out of its coop and Micky came running, yelling at the top of his lungs, "He's chasing me; he'll bite me. I'm afraid. I'm afraid."

"Now, darling," you assured him. "You're a big boy and big boys aren't afraid of little rabbits" [denying the feelings he has expressed].

Finally, all is calm. Jane is playing with her doll and doll buggy. Micky is sitting on the back steps with a big hunk of plasticine. You feel that self-satisfied, in-control feeling for a few moments. But all of a sudden you notice that Micky is glaring and that Jane has appropriated more than two-thirds of his clay. Micky's whole body is tensed for combat, but his keen little mind sees the hazards of attacking bigger Jane. So instead of letting his fists do the job, he lets a teasing tongue do it for him. He sings in rising crescendo:

> Jane, Jane
> Gives me a pain.
> Kick her like a mooly moo;
> Smear her up with doodledoo . . .

You steel yourself and say patiently and with long-tried endurance, "Don't you know, Jane, you're not to grab from Micky. And don't you know, Micky, that it's not nice to talk to your sister like that?"

"But," Jane stamps her foot, "I need the clay for doll food."

"Don't argue, Jane."

"She took my clay," wails Micky, stepping in when he feels the advantage on his side.

"Now stop it, children. Give the clay back, Jane. And tell Jane you're sorry, Micky."

And then you pause. You can make Jane give back the clay. But you know from past experience that in a little while her mean feelings toward Micky will come out again in some other way. You can make Micky apologize. But if he does,

132

he'll be denying his true feelings. You'll be encouraging him to lie.

"Oh dear," you sigh, utterly dejected.

That was the old you. Here is the new. We'll roll back the reel and start the afternoon over.

Micky comes sobbing, "Jane's rabbit'll bite me. I'm afraid."

"I know how it feels to be afraid, dear," you say, accepting his feelings. And you put an arm around him and wait to hear more.

"I wanna have that old rabbit drowned in the fishpond. He's an old stinky like Jane."

Astonished, you can manage no more than to echo. "You think he's an old stinky like Jane."

"Uh-huh!" with great gusto and a smile through the tears.

"There!" you think to yourself. "Even if I stumbled I did get to his feelings. I let him know I understood and accepted them."

Contentedly you turn back to your knitting. But in a moment comes the fiasco with Jane taking Micky's clay and Micky singing his teasing verse.

You put down your needles and look up sagely. "Seems to me, you're feeling real mean to each other," you put into words the feelings they have shown. "Give Micky his clay, Jane." You have to stop certain actions. "And now let's see what you can do to get the mean feelings out in some other way."

They stare at you curiously. They've never seen you act like this!

"Jane, suppose you play that your doll is Micky. Then you'll be able to do whatever you want to him. And, Micky, suppose you make a clay Jane and do whatever you want to her."

They get the idea readily. Jane scolds her doll and spanks him. Micky pinches the clay and grinds it under his feet. You nod every once in a while and comment, "Jane wants to be mean to Micky and Micky wants to be mean to Jane."

After a while you hear Micky pick up his chant: "Jane, Jane, wet her in the rain . . . Jane, Jane, doodledoo's her name . . . Kick her like a mooly moo; smear her up with doodledoo. . . ." He runs on and on, ad-libbing.

Then you notice Jane has stopped in her tracks and is

"Don't worry, Sis. I'll apologize later."

listening to Micky with a rapt look on her face—a kind of kinship. Suddenly she grins her toothless grin. "Oh Micky, really! You're the muddlinest, puddinest, pinniest pinhead."

Their eyes meet and they burst into peals of laughter. "You're funny!" says Micky with real appreciation of Jane's humor.

"Uh-huh," says Jane, with a bit of condescension. But in a moment she adds generously, "You're funny too!"

They laugh again and you laugh with them, wondering why you'd thought a while back that life was so grim.

Almost every little girl reaches a stage in her life, around four or five, where she wants to be married to her daddy. Almost every little boy feels the same way about being his mother's husband.

"When I grow up I'm going to marry my mom!" . . . "When I get big I'm going to be my daddy's best wife." Most of us have heard our children make comments like this. We listen and smile and think, "How cute!" as long as the rivalry aspect does not emerge. But whenever a child shows that he would like to be rid of a parent in order to step into his shoes, then we react in quite another way. Then we are apt to become horrified or angry. And yet, such feelings are natural too.

Jim, just five, shows this. He says, "Isn't it a nuisance to have a father live in our house?"

"Sometimes you'd like daddy not to live here," his mother answers his feelings.

"Yes. Then I'd be the daddy to you."

"You'd like to be my husband?"

"Yes." But quickly relenting, he adds, "We could have daddy for our little boy."

Mabel is more adamant. "Let's tell mother to go 'way. Then we can be just us," she proposes to her father.

"You'd like mother to be gone so there'd be just the two of us."

"Uh-huh. And we won't let her come in the house anymore. We'll shut the door tight and we'll let her ring and ring and ring and knock and knock. We won't listen nohow."

Peter's designs are bolder and bloodier. "My daddy's leaving on the train tonight," he confides to the delivery man, making the story up out of whole cloth. "It's a bad train. The men are going to kill him. And the train is going to get wrecked. Then I'll be the daddy here."

After the man is gone Peter's mother nods sagely. "I know

135

how it is, Peter. Sometimes you like to make up how daddy won't be here anymore. Then you could have mother all to yourself."

It's important to be very tolerant and understanding of our children at this stage. If a mother is harsh or if a father pushes away a small daughter who is too demanding, the child may easily come to feel two things: "I never want to grow into a woman like mother" and "I never want to marry a man like father." The same thing holds for a boy.

On the other hand, where a parent is too flattered, too pleased, too amused; where he encourages the love-making or plays up to it—he also raises difficulties. For then the attachment is apt to remain beyond its day and the child has a hard time growing out of it.

If handled acceptantly and in a matter-of-fact, gentle way, the child will outgrow the rivalry with mother or father in the natural course of events. A boy will want to grow as tall as daddy and as strong. He will want to wear the same kind of shirt and blue jeans and walk with the same stride. He will, around nine, admire his father's knowledge and want to share in his skills, become a carpenter with him, throw a ball as he does. His swagger says, "We're men together," and his scowl may add, "Let's throw those pesky women out!" A girl around the same age will want to have dresses like mother's. She will want to go out into the kitchen with mother and baste and bake . . . When the day for such identification comes, neither a harsh nor an idealized picture from an earlier time will stand in the way.

Jealousies and rivalries are natural. Within the family a child has practice in living vigorously if we let him. Here is where he learns first to claim a loved one. Here is where he learns that moments of winning and moments of yielding can balance in the long run. But most important, here he learns to accept and understand others by virtue of his being accepted and understood.

136

9. He wants to be big and bigger

TESTING HIMSELF OUT

After a child passes through the first crucial years, when mammoth events seem concentrated into such a short space of time, he settles down in a steadier fashion to the business of growing up. All through his childhood and adolescence the push is in him to become a person who can stand on his own. Yet he must still lean and depend on his parents. But, at the same time, bit by bit, he must separate himself and become independent. For him this constitutes a major achievement. To accomplish it, he must test himself out. He must pit himself against others. He must assert himself. He must try his own wings.

We, his parents, want him to do this. We know that we won't always be with him. We know that growing up is a long, slow business. We know that the *achievement of independence* is essential if he is to take his place in our rough, tough, troubled world. We know he must have courage of both body and mind if he is to survive and help others to survive. He must have stalwartness if he is to lend his brain and brawn to shaping society into more generous proportions.

We know, too, that our job in relation to his growing up is not easy. We cannot leave him to blunder hopelessly in ignorance. We cannot leave him completely alone to make errors which may be irreparable. We need to stay with him and support him physically, mentally, morally. *We must steer his growth into maturity but we must not obstruct it.* We need to guide him, give him precepts and examples to follow. We must stand by, ready to step in wherever we are needed. But all along we must also give him opportunities to

"Tell me, Mother. Could Psychology help me to be attractive to older men of nineteen or twenty?"

feel his own strength. He will do much that displeases us. And yet, we must endure with him in his attempts to be big and bigger even though he often tries to be bigger than he is.

"It's hard for me to keep from stepping in where I'm not really needed," said ten-year-old Sheila's mother. "I keep feeling 'she has to be shown' when she really is quite capable and wants to handle things for herself. For instance, the other day when I got home she was in the kitchen baking a cake. She'd found a recipe herself and was starting to spoon in the flour without sifting it. I could hardly keep my hands off. I wanted to say, 'Here, let me show you!' But I caught

138

myself just in time, remembering how in the past when I'd said, 'Do it this way!' she'd sulked and argued and fought that her way was best.

"I told myself if I hadn't come home at just this moment she would have carried through on her own . . . I let her be. And, so help me, if that cake didn't turn out perfectly delicious. I don't see how, but it did!"

Sheila's mother paused a moment, reflectively. "The best part of it was Sheila's face. It shone. I didn't even mind when she said with great superiority, 'There, Mother, you see you didn't have to interfere. This is better than any cake *you* ever made!'"

To Sheila, the cake-baking in itself apparently did not seem achievement enough. She wanted not only to be big enough to bake it. She wanted also to be bigger than her mother to prove that she was big.

All along as a child grows, the business of testing himself out against things seems insufficient. In addition, *he must test himself out against people.* This is an essential for him. It is a necessity if he is to become a strong person instead of a weakling and a yes man.

THE ATOMIC ADOLESCENT

Because he is unskilled in putting himself forward, his attempts at independence often take the form of argumentativeness and defiance. As he approaches adolescence he is apt to be dominating and bossy. He wants his own way and demands it. He belittles us and lifts himself. He boasts to show that he is bigger than big. He exaggerates. He tries to put things over. He is rude and unheeding. He quarrels and fights with his friends. When he can't get by and win on fair terms, he cheats. And continuously, he protests and tries to shake off supervision to show that he is able to decide for himself and do things on his own.

All of this puts us in a difficult spot. For we who are his parents are the most accessible, most available people against whom he can try his strength. We are also stamped in his mind as those who have always tried to "down" him.

If we grow too harsh with him, if we make it too hard for him to try his bigness out against us, then resentment is apt to get mixed up with his desire to be big. We threaten him in the drive for one of the very greatest achievements he must accomplish in life—the ability to stand on his own.

If we defeat him, another thing happens: he turns elsewhere and finds substitute people against whom to pit himself. He may, for instance, be rude to his grandparents as substitutes for us. He may grow disrespectful and disobedient to his teachers. Or he may pick on servants or on people whom he believes are easy targets, as Negroes or Italians, Catholics, Jews. . . .

If we are wise, we prefer to give him chances to test his bigness against us. If his teachers are wise, they will help us in the schools.* For, if school and home both give him chances to work off the negative parts of feeling bigger, the positive parts will enter more quickly and will permit him to be big in more productive, more creative and more social ways.

All along we will be helped to do what is best for a child if we can remember this:

What we call adolescent
DISOBEDIENCE is often nothing
more than a child's NORMAL
GROWTH TOWARD INDEPENDENCE

IRRESOLUTE REVOLUTIONISTS

The adolescent's rebellion is often an echo of the small child's plaintive lament.

* See Chapter 14.

140

I'm not a PERSON
I'm a little girl;
But someday
I'll be a person
Like you.

Throughout many of his disobedient moments it's as if the adolescent were saying, "I'm trying to get the best of you so that I can feel myself big enough to be a person." Underneath, however, he may feel a woeful lack of confidence in his own ability to steer himself. The swaggering bravado, the oversure pronouncements, the argumentativeness, the ardent belittling of our fondest beliefs may all add up to an attempt to cover his uncertainty. He swishes his tail and roars like a lion in order to cover that he is a mouse.

On the one hand, because we think his mind has grown older and more mature, we expect him to behave in a more docile fashion. We expect him virtually to be a better child, to carry out the little-boy or little-girl obedience more completely. On the other hand, because his body is bigger, we expect him to do bigger things. We expect him to be more cooperative and tidy. To be more dependable, to help us more regularly with the chores without constant reminding. We expect him to clean out the garbage, help mother do the dishes, help father wash the car, take on the mowing of the lawn, the feeding of the pets.

"I wish I had something to say about choosing what I'm to do since I have to do it," says Enid, fifteen. "They yell, 'Do this. Do that. And do it properly!' . . . They expect results like a grownup's. But they treat me like a child."

Roland's complaint is somewhat different. "They expect me to do it in a certain way at a certain time. I don't mind doing the dishes if I can do them later on in the evening. But right after supper's the time I *have* to go out and play ball with the gang. Honestly, I don't mind cooperating. I don't

141

even mind being told, though I'd rather be asked. But I do mind being *nagged*."

Where cooperation is a living word in a family, the children are more apt to fall in with the rest.

Sixteen-year-old Emily is all agog. "It's neat going over to Pat's. Her mother *lets* her cook the dinner. All alone. She has one night a week and that's *her* night. She arranges the menu and does the marketing and looks up the recipes and everything. Just as if it were her own home. They all have their nights. Even Pat's father. He's a wonderful chef. He lets Pat's kid brother share his night sometimes. They cook the weirdest things. But it's fun."

Twelve-year-old Andy is just as enthusiastic over helping the neighbor wash the car. "But will he help me?" complains his father. "Not on your life."

Andy himself describes the difference. "Gee, when I help Mr. Smith he says, 'Swell, Andy!' He listens to my suggestions and once he even took one. But my dad keeps picking. 'Hurry up, Andy!' . . . 'Don't do it that way!' . . . 'What kind of a job is *that?*' Nothing's ever good enough . . ."

In our homes, far too often cooperation and coercion get all mixed up. Then a child is apt to rebel. Or he may rebel, not because of the things we impose on the present, but because of the load he bore in the past before we knew what we know. Again it becomes a matter of managing the resentment and anger that stand behind every child's "won'ts."

Says Eric, thirteen, "I won't be a sissy. I won't wash the dishes. Just try and make me." He wears a belligerent, I'll-dare-you-to air.

His mother reflects his feelings with kindly accord and an easy twinkle of humor. "You feel he-men don't do such jobs."

Says Eric back fast, "Okay. Okay," he says, still grumbling. And then, with a flash of humor all his own, he adds, "It's no

142

use both of us getting hot and bothered. I'll do it if you mind me and get out of my way."

The issue is settled. The conflict is by-passed. Eric has had something to say about how he should carry through. He has regained his status and self-esteem.

But no issue can be settled once and for all. In these years of growing, the same sort of behavior keeps cropping up again and again until a child finally passes from childhood into a more adult stage.

Where a child is developing normally and in a healthy fashion, there should be moments of accord as well as moments of struggle throughout the days and years. Where defiance keeps rising, where it mounts to proportions that seem to override everything else, we can be sure we're not dealing alone with the wish for independence. We can be sure that our child has added to this wish a lot of anger for hurts he feels in the present or has felt in the past.

We will have to deal with his anger, then, as well as with his wish for bigness. By now we know the essential principles and procedures in accomplishing this. We know, for one thing, that if a child is already angry and that if we then push and prod and punish him, either through body or browbeatings, his anger will grow. He may improve in this or that small bit of behavior, but the badness will come out somewhere else. His resentment will mount and will appear in disguised ways, if not in exaggerated revolt.

When our child was around nine or ten, he already began to ally himself with other children against us. This continued while he approached his teens. Even though he quarreled with his friends, even though he fought them, discarded them, picked them up anew, still he seemed to have a strange sort of capacity for hitching up with them to form a combine to combat us. He seemed to choose the worst and toughest among them and to relish, and be intrigued by, their very

143

wildest side. They tumbled all over the house, a bunch of rowdies. They ganged up. They ran all over the newly planted flower beds. They played ball on the street. They were invariably off somewhere when it was time for dinner. But worst of all, our youngster held the other youngsters' parents up to us as examples of what parents should be. *Their* parents let them go to so-and-so many shows a week; so why shouldn't we? They let their kids stay up till all hours; so why shouldn't we? "Tom's folks never care what time he comes in; they save dinner for him." . . . "They don't make him practice." . . . "They let him listen to the radio as late as he wants." . . . "They let him have whatever he likes for his lunch! Three ice-cream cones and four lollipops! And they don't care if he doesn't eat anything else."

We may have begun to wonder whether we've chosen our neighbors rashly. But were we to move we would find that another district yielded the selfsame results.

As our children grow on into their teens, the wilder physical rowdiness is replaced by an equally supercilious, I-know-it-all air. Other boys and girls are held up as the arbiters of custom and knowledge. We may shout, "I don't care what the other boys or girls do or think; you'll do as we say."

We may plead for more reasonable compliance. We may fuss and fume, only to be met with a disdainful and arrogant response which tells us that we know nothing and are, in fact, no bigger than worms.

Often such attack on us is to ward off what our child feels as an attack on him—an attack on his status, on his ability to achieve on his own.

Ragan was sixteen, a tall, well-built boy who passed easily as eighteen. His mother complained to the psychologist, saying, "The trouble is over the car. He swears at us and reviles us because we won't let him use it at night. We know nothing, he says. We're nitwits; we're dumb. . . ."

"Yes," his father assented.

"Tell about the other day." His mother urged his father on. "What Ragan said about my being old-fashioned. . . ."

"Yes," nodded his father. "He got so fresh. He said, 'The trouble with you, old lady, is that you're trying to put the new look on a 1910 chassis.'"

Their complaints ran on and on.

So did Ragan's. "My mother's impossible," he stated. "She doesn't want me to have any life of my own. She has to pick my friends according to her social register. If I bring anyone home she invariably finds fault. Something's always wrong. I can't bring a girl to the house and have her picked on. I *have* to have the car so I can take her out.

"And another thing. My mother wants to drag me along to all her friends'. But they don't want me any more than I want to go. They think I'm a freak trotting along with her like a little kid.

"And when we're home alone it's talk, talk, talk: Why won't I go to the 'select' boy's school she's got picked? She doesn't like the school I want to go to. I'll get into the wrong company, she says, meaning kids whose folks have no Bradstreet rating. It's disgusting, I tell you. I need the car to get away.

"My father would be better if he had some guts. But he hasn't. He's nothing but a yes man. He's her shadow. He wouldn't dare stick up for another guy. I'll be darned if I'll just sit and take it and become *that* kind of a man. If she won't give me the car so I can get out and get some peace, I'll go steal one. . . ."

The car had become the hub around which the battle raged. But, actually, the battle was over quite another item. It was over Ragan's independence.

When his father and mother saw this and when they learned something about the new ways in discipline, many things changed.

"I've made a lot of mistakes," his mother told Ragan. "I'd

be just as mad as you've been if anybody tried to choose my friends. I'm turning over a new leaf. I'm going to do better!"

"Seeing is believing!" Ragan countered.

"You don't quite trust me," his mother reflected. "And I can't say I blame you. I may slip, I know."

"Gee, Mom, everybody makes mistakes. I'll tell you if you do slip!" And a shy little smile came across Ragan's face.

For months Ragan caught the slips with quick-flashing resentment. "There you go again, Mother. Picking on my new girl friend. What if she does wear gold slippers and a woolen skirt. That's the way all the kids do. Don't be an old tortoise. Open your eyes. . . ."

"You hate me to criticize her," his mother sheepishly mirrored what she thought Ragan felt.

"I sure do. It makes me so mad!"

Then father said, reflecting Ragan's feelings, "You feel mother's trying to take away your right to choose a girl for yourself!"

"That's it, Dad. You put your finger right on it. . . ."

"Or my foot right into it," with a wry smile at his wife's angry look. "I'm making you mad, dear. . . ."

"You're worse than Ragan. I don't know where I'm at with both of you men asserting independence all at once."

Both his father and mother, however, remained firm on the issue of the car. But, strangely, this issue grew less and less intense. As time wore on the battles grew fewer. Ragan's mother improved in her ability to mirror and accept Ragan's direct resentment to her. And Ragan talked more and more freely about how he felt. Ragan's father not only accepted his son's feelings; he gave him more manly support by being more manly. By virtue of his own shift to greater assertiveness, he made Ragan less afraid of becoming a yes man. Moreover, since he had a friend in court, Ragan no longer needed to fight two enemies. He could relax a little. Then, as his mother learned more and more to let Ragan choose his own friends

146

and his own school, as she let down on trying to regulate his life as if he were six instead of sixteen—Ragan found he had two friends. Since both his parents were ready and willing to accept his feelings, he didn't need to press them to accept every action. Nor did he have to stay their enemy to prove himself.

These adolescent children of ours need our help in growing into independence, not our hindrance.

> Wherever an adolescent is able
> to make choices or decisions
> or to accomplish things
> ON HIS OWN
> we should give him the chance.

This doesn't mean, however, that we should force him into premature independence. We should give him all the help and support he needs from us, remembering that in spite of his revolt he is still irresolute. But our help should be aimed at making him feel more capable rather than less capable of functioning on his own. Our help should be aimed at making him feel bigger and better and more able to take over. It should not be directed at tearing him down in order to force obedience on him for discipline's sake.

THE GANGSTER TO THE FORE

During adolescence even more than earlier we need to watch ourselves lest we press and prod and punish beyond a child's endurance. For, if we make our load of requirements and forbiddings too heavy, then perfectly normal attempts at independence may turn into more pronounced or into even abnormal revolt.

Ordinarily, in his early teens, our child will admire and sing paeans of praise to the more aggressive youngsters. This is a sort of wish that he too could be great enough to be as sinister and as well able to bring aggression out. If our

147

pressure grows too heavy, he may even gang up with delinquents and get into scrapes. He may pilfer. He may join in gang warfare. Or, less blatantly, he may turn the gangster impulses against himself and murder his own abilities and strengths, remaining weak, accomplishing little, living up to none of his potentialities. He may feel misunderstood, as if he were an adopted child rather than really ours. He may grow morose and develop a brooding sense of isolation.

Or—more normally—he may use his normal adolescent streaks of tiredness as a club against us. "I'm too tired to go to the store, Ma" . . . "Gee, Dad, I can't help mow the lawn today. My legs ache I'm so dead." Or he may go back to some of his baby ways of letting the madness come to the fore.

Children, as they start developing and turning from child into man or woman, use a lot of energy for physical growing. Their appetites increase apace in order to supply the extra food they need for the bodily changes that are taking place inside and out. The youngster with overaggressive impulses may now grab food and devour it with a kind of cannibalistic ferocity and with a return to baby emphasis on mouth and lips for satisfaction. He hurts himself by growing fat and ungainly and he hurts his parents as well.

All children, at this same stage, are more or less messy. Some children, however, now go back to exaggerated messing, particularly those who had no chance to live out their messing at an earlier day. Not only will their rooms show the usual disregard for tidiness, not only will their dress be unkempt and their faces unwashed, but all kinds of filth may be dragged and left to mildew and decay. "He nauseates me, he's so filthy," said one twelve-year-old boy's mother. He was revolting through a return to baby dirtiness. Quite obviously he was letting out his piled-up aggression.

During all these manifestations we need to remember one thing above all. Normally a child wants to grow up. He wants to emancipate himself. He will struggle to earn his rights of independence.

As we firmly accept his feelings and say them back to him understandingly, many a storm blows past. We can mirror what he feels by saying, for example, "I know you want to show me that you can do it your way." . . . "I know you'd rather plan how to do it yourself." . . . "You don't like my interference," or "You're mad because you think I'm trying to take over" . . . "You don't want me to boss you" . . . "You hate me to tell you to do things, I know."

Our tone of voice and the feelings we have behind it will be of prime importance. We can say what we say in lip service rather than in true acceptance. Behind the words our child will then feel an aggrieved sort of tenseness. Or we can say what we say with real acceptance—loving him and feeling *with* him, understanding that the struggle for grownupness is frought with far more turmoil for him than for us.

THE COMPLEXITIES OF SEX
AND THE BOY-GIRL BUSINESS

Essentially, we want our children to grow up sturdily and to become the fine men and women who can take their places in the world and lead happy, well-adjusted lives. That's why we want to become aware of attitudes in ourselves that may impede their progress. That's why we want also to understand enough of our children's psychological as well as physical development to guide them wisely through the formative years. Much as we hate to lose our children, much as we love their dependency on us, we want ultimately to see them free of us and steering themselves. To this end we will try to help them get rid of feelings that may stand in the way of their growing up.

In the transition from childhood into manhood, every individual must achieve selfhood, a sense of his own identity as a big enough and a worth-while enough person to take his

149

place in the world. He must also learn to relate himself to other people with sturdy fellowship, with loyal consideration, without too many feelings of resentment and enmity piled up and blocking the way. Furthermore, for his fullest happiness, he will want to achieve the ultimate ability to share life and love with another human being—a husband or wife. He must learn to accept his sexual impulses as right and fine and a part of this sharing of life and of love.

In all the phases of his development, he is bound to be inept and fumbling as he grows. He must work through negative feelings in order to gain positive ones. He must pass through immature stages in order at long last to become mature.

Boy-girl relationships are no exception. Here, too, much ineptness and immaturity and fumbling occur.

"My twelve-year-old girl is so silly with her giggling nonsense!" says one mother disgustedly.

"My twelve-year-old boy is so snooty to girls, I could kill him. He thinks they're beneath his notice. He mutters disgustedly when his sister has her friends over. And yet, he sticks like a leech and teases them from morning till night."

At twelve and thirteen and on till about fourteen or fifteen, the differences in their height alone make for difficulties between boys and girls. The girl is ordinarily taller and more developed than the boy during these years. In consequence, she looks on him disdainfully as "a little shrimp," makes herself as uniformly pretty as every other girl of her age, titters in shy and embarrassed fashion at the older boys or sticks up her nose sedately, protesting disinterest, yet hoping hopelessly that they will turn her way. But they are past noticing her. And so, feeling turned down, she must seek some defense.

Thirteen-year-old Marlene states all this in her own fashion. "I'm not anti-boys," she says primly. "But what's a girl like me to do? Those little freaks at school literally smell. I wouldn't be seen with one of them on a bet. There are some

150

older boys, though, who are just beautiful—with shoulders and all that. Only they think they're supermen or something much too big. But why should I care? If they had any sense they'd see that I know how to love. I've been true to Gregory Peck now for years!"

In his way, thirteen-year-old John finds life with the opposite sex fraught with problems. "Girls!" he sneers. "All they want is for you to play post office with them or buy them candy bars!" He avows repeatedly that he will have nothing whatsoever to do with them until finally he bares his soul. "There's one little honey," he expounds with a whistle. And then with return to crestfallenness, he finishes by saying, "She's in love, though, with an older man about eighteen. So what's a guy like me to do?"

To these boys and girls, this is serious and defeating business. They want acceptance. They need to know that we don't condemn their feeling that "Girls are a nuisance!" or that "Boys are pests!" "Yes," mirrored twelve-year-old Anne's mother acceptantly, "women do have their troubles with men!"

At this age, children's size and developmental incompatibilities raise hazards. These combine, in turn, with another hazard that seems even harder to bear, namely, the stirring of sex that pushes to the fore with adolescent growth.

We do not ordinarily realize that in the boy puberal changes may start as early as nine, though they usually do not begin till between ten and a half and thirteen. In the girl they may start as early as eight, though again, they more ordinarily begin between nine and twelve. Inner glandular changes take place before any external, physical changes are perceived and before the onset of menstruation in the girl or seminal emissions in the boy.

With the increased development come increased sexual feelings. But these are not the first pleasurable bodily sensations a child has had, nor are his reactions to them his first reactions to the whole problem of sex with which he must

151

cope as he matures. Perhaps, much earlier, when he was a baby he got bodily sensations of pleasure from a thumb and we condemned him. Perhaps he got pleasure from elimination and again we condemned him. Perhaps, as many small children do, he snuggled up to a parent's body like a little, sexy animal, and without even realizing it, we withdrew from him and condemned him for this. Perhaps we caught him in sex play with some little companion and told him he was wicked and bad. Or, perhaps, in a way that is almost universal, he discovered that he could get pleasurable feelings from touching himself and we raised our hands in horror and felt that he was beyond repair.

Even babies and very small children show that they are aware of pleasant sensations in their genitals by touching themselves. Because we have been taught in our own childhood that this is dangerous and detrimental, we are apt to make a child afraid that he may injure his body in this manner and do himself untold harm.

Many old wives' tales are still current about this matter of masturbation. They are untrue. We have enough scientific evidence today to know with assurance that masturbation does no harm. It does not injure health in any way. Even if carried to extremes it never makes a person crazy or weak or ill. Nor does it affect sexual potency. But we also know that when a child grows anxious and worried and afraid over it, the anxiety, worry and fear *can* do him harm.

If a child masturbates in place of enjoying activities and companionship, the practice may be a sign that he has been hurt in some way and is using his body to comfort himself. Then we must see that the cause of his hurt is removed. If he masturbates openly and with a kind of aggressive exhibitionism, he may be using the practice to express his anger through aggravating or shocking those who catch him. Then we have to remove the cause of his anger. But attacking the masturbation itself does no good, only harm.

152

Many parents not knowing that masturbation is harmless say and do the very things that put anxiety and worry and fear into their children's heads.

"If you keep on with that you'll injure your health." . . . "You'll make yourself sick." . . . "You'll hurt yourself." These are common remarks. Also common are threats of punishment designed to make children stop, when actually nothing short of scaring them into a panic can *make* them stop. On the other hand, they will stop of their own accord when they have grown out of it, just as they have stopped earlier, immature forms of gaining bodily pleasure. It's worse than useless—it's terrifying—to say, as did one father, "If you don't stop, I'll have to get the doctor to cut it off."

Timothy, nine, went into a panic when he was sent to the hospital to have his tonsils removed. Later, the truth came out. He was petrified lest, when he went under the anesthetic, the doctor would somehow know what he had been doing and would take this opportunity to punish him as he deserved.

Dana lived in constant terror of "If I don't stop, and I can't stop, it will shrivel and fall off!" Edward confided that he would be so crippled that he would have to wear a brace. Violet muttered through her tears, "I think they cut part of me off—once when I was little—to punish me and make me good. But it didn't help."

More subtle but equally frightening are warnings that a child will not grow up properly or that he will not be able to have children or make a normal marriage.

Even where threats and warnings are not made openly and a parent subtly suggests such things as "Hands out from under the covers," a child senses the adult attitude. If fear exists in the adult's mind, it is caught by the child.

In adolescence when sexual stirrings are heightened, all the fears which were felt in connection with earlier stirrings are also heightened. These come in conflict with the child's need to be big, capable and worth while and with his need

153

to make a good adjustment to the opposite sex. He is not only frightened that his body may be injured or incapacitated. He fears also that he will remain weak and inferior and that no one of the opposite sex will find him desirable.

To make things even worse, he doesn't dare confide in anyone. If he tells his parents, they will only condemn him more and make things harder to bear.

Fourteen-year-old Sandra was more fortunate than most youngsters. One day she blurted out to her mother, "I'm impossible." She went on, sobbing, "I can't help it, Mom. I make a good resolution and then I go on and on. I'm no good. I know it. I'm wicked. I'll never have any babies. No man will ever want to marry me. Oh, Mom, how can anyone love me? I'm so ashamed."

"I know it, darling," Sandra's mother replied, a small tightness creeping up inside her. Could she carry this through? She had learned only recently what the facts were! "I know how you feel, Sandy," she reiterated. And then, she added bravely, "I used to feel the same way myself."

"Mo-ther!" Sandra sat bolt upright. Her look was concocted of incredulity and grave disapproval. "Mo-ther, you didn't?"

In recalling the event later, Sandra's mother recounted, "What could I do but put back my head and laugh? Sandy laughed, too, and the horror was gone."

Ten-year-old Wilder's mother handled another sort of evidence of sexual stirrings with equal sensitivity and acceptance.

"I looked out the window one day," she said, "and I noticed that Wilder and three of the neighborhood children were crawling into the big doghouse in the back yard. They'd tacked a blanket over the entrance. The first thing I knew out came a shoe. Out came another shoe. A sock. Another sock. Sweaters. Shirts.

"Ye gods! I thought. What goes on? 'Wilder!' I called.

"After a few moments a subdued child appeared, half-dressed.

154

" 'What on earth are you doing?'

"He shifted from one foot to the other, embarrassed, 'We're playing a new game, Ma. We're playing *poor*.'

"I guess I looked dumb or something, because he went on to explain, 'Like poor people, Ma. They don't have any clothes.'

"Well, I evicted the 'poor' quietly from the doghouse and after they had gone their respective ways, I said to Wilder, 'You know, dear, about that game. You were feeling a little embarrassed!'

" 'Uh-huh!' he admitted, crestfallen. 'You see, Ma, we were kind of experimenting . . . with—oh well—sort of nice feelings. . . .'

" 'I know, son! All children have sex feelings. They are nice feelings. But children don't experiment with other children to get them. It just isn't done!'

" 'You mean,' he said with positive emphasis, 'you wait till you're married!' " And that settled the "poor" game once and for all.

As with many other issues, we may need to go into ourselves first, before we handle the thing with our children. We may need to ask ourselves, "How do I feel about this matter? Can I be frank enough to say, for instance, 'I've made a mistake in warning you that there's danger in touching yourself? There isn't. Lots of people do it. Actually, it does no harm!'

"Am I clear enough to realize that I have a task before me far more important than clinging to old wives' tales and taboos? It's the task of freeing my child of fear which otherwise could ruin the sense of his own good identity, leave him doubting that anyone could want him and wondering whether he had the right, the power or the strength to grow up!"

Parents are frequently worried that adolescent boys and girls will go too far in their petting, that they will get into scrapes. Many times the girl or boy who gets into the greatest difficulties, however, is the very one who has been most carefully guarded and watched.

"They won't let me have any evening dates," announced sixteen-year-old Annette, "unless there's an older couple along or unless they're with me. If I go to a dance I have to be called for. I'm allowed to go to a movie with a girl but not with a boy, and I have to be home by eleven-thirty. They're suspicious that something terrible is going to happen. Well, if they don't watch out it will! With their old-fashioned ideas, they think that everything sexy goes on after dark. But I've been sneaking my dates in the daytime and, believe me, just as much can go on then."

Annette's relationship with a boy was something to be used as a club against her parents. Through sexual escapades she expressed her hostility. She took this aggressive, unhappy way to make herself big. Her parents' overstrictness had made resentment mount in her till she had lost the natural reserve and sense of morality that most youngsters of Annette's age possess in spite of superficial sophistication.

A FORWARD LOOK

In the adolescent years—as earlier—

No matter how much we've tried to give of every emotional satisfaction he needs, let's try harder. Let's try to supply our child with more love and appreciation, more chances to be big, more chances to be himself and, at one and the same time, to feel that he belongs and is wanted.

Let's examine ourselves to find how great a load of orders and forbiddings and demands we are putting on him and let's reduce it as much as we can.

Let's count the rules we're imposing and cut out the unessential ones.

Let's give him opportunities to steer himself, to choose his own way of doing things, to make his own choices in so far as he is able. But let's not require more in the way of independence than he is ready to achieve.

Let's try really to get *his* point of view and to understand and accept his feelings.

Let's keep on mirroring his feelings to show him we do understand.

Let's give him opportunities galore to drain out the poison, to get the "bad" feelings out so that the good ones may have more room to expand in.

Remember, when enough of the revolt is out, the positive, cooperative feelings flow in to fill the gap. But it usually takes a while before enough of the revolt is actually drained.

Whether or not our child is adolescent—no matter what age he is—let's remember: He is progressively growing. He needs all along to feel able to achieve what he can on his own. But he must not be pressed beyond this.

So let's—

TRY THE NEW WAYS IN DISCIPLINE FOR SIX MONTHS AT LEAST or a year. REALLY TRY THEM.

As is often the case, our child grows particularly disobedient when we inaugurate our new regime. If so, as emergency measure let's cut down and *relax every possible request* for about a week. Then we can very gradually put the most important ones back. Jotting down each thing we ask as we ask it gives us insight into how many things we are asking and which ones we can curtail.

One thing more; and this is a new one and an extremely important one:

Let's provide for RELEASE OF
EMOTIONS AT OTHER THAN AT TROUBLED TIMES.

Up to now we have talked of letting a child get the poison out when he is angry or disturbed. We have counted on continuous explosions and fights and disobedience to provide release of the unwanted feelings. But these are not enough! We need to provide additional opportunities for the troubled feelings to come out. There can be pleasant times when feelings are aired; not only unpleasant ones.

At the very beginning of this book certain activities were mentioned which can do a great deal in preventing and reducing disciplinary ills. They are not necessarily tumultuous, unhappy activities. They can be part of playtimes and fun.

The next section of this book tells how to provide such activities. After we have read it and have inaugurated them into our daily living and have given them a good try, we'll probably find that our children do not seem so driven toward disobedience. For we will have given them happier times of play and accord in which to bring their feelings out.

Part Three

What you can do in times of peace to reduce times of stress

10. Time alone together

A child must share so much of us with chores and with other people that he frequently feels we do not want to spend time with him.

"You've got time for everything else but me," complained seven-year-old Clara. "You've got time for the telephone and time for the market and time for cooking and time for daddy and the baby and your friends. But none for me."

"Why Clara!" answered her mother indignantly, "I spend lots of time with you. Don't I help you dress every morning?"

"Yes," came the answer quickly. And then Clara brought out a surprising thing. "But that time doesn't count. It belongs to the clothes!"

"Don't I eat with you?"

"Yes. But that time doesn't count either. It belongs to the food—or to daddy."

"Don't I read to you?"

"Yes. But you attend to the book then. Not to me."

"It suddenly dawned," recounted Clara's mother. "Clara's right. When I help her dress I'm focusing on the clothes—getting them out, checking buttons, seeing that they go on straight. When I'm at the table with her, I'm dividing myself between attending to serving, talking with her father and doing a million and one little things. I can hear myself interrupting her chatter with my urgings for her to finish. No wonder she says this time belongs to the food. She's right, too, about when I read. I'm following the story and focusing on it. There's actually no time during the day when I'm focusing entirely on her.

"I imagine she feels much as I feel when I'm getting dressed to go out and am late and Charles sits around and keeps urging me to hurry. I don't feel that he's spending time with me. I discount it. It isn't really time together. He's pummeling

Sonny Boy: "You take this and eat it right now and quickly, and stop going to the ice-box in between meals like you always do."

at me and I feel out of rapport. I guess Clara feels the same way about the time I spend with her."

Most of us believe we spend ample time with our children and no doubt we do. *But it isn't the right sort of time.* Far too much of it is *supervisory* time, taken up with urgings and proddings and giving orders, with our focus on what needs to be done rather than on the child himself. As Clara implied, such time does not bring the feeling of togetherness into being. It does not satisfy a child. It belongs to *things,* not to *him.*

Another frequent difficulty lies in the fact that people

can spend time in close physical proximity without any emotional closeness. They can be side by side and yet not feel that sense of belonging together that all of us crave.

"Let's do something together!" says one young wife, pleadingly.

"Now look, dear, be sensible. We've been together all evening."

"But you've been reading the paper and I've been doing crossword puzzles and that's not the same thing at all. I want to enjoy time *with* you, not only *alongside* you!"

Children feel just this way. They crave time *with* us, not just in our company. They crave time in which we are focused entirely on them. Not on making them mind. Not on making them do things. They crave time when we are not involved with other activities or with other people. Time which is their *time alone*.

YOUR TIME ALONE

Much disciplinary difficulty can be avoided if a child is given the sort of time he craves. Having us all to himself for even short periods with focus completely on him helps him to know that we love him. It helps him to feel that he belongs.

Some parents, understanding this, have inaugurated into the course of their day a separate *time alone* for each child. They make this a time when "minding" and supervision are forgotten words and where attention to everything but the child himself is shut off.

"At first I thought it would be too hard to arrange," said one mother. "But I've found that even fifteen minutes a day does such wonders that it's well worth while. I don't know any single thing that has reduced our disciplinary problems so much."

When a child knows that he has a certain time coming to him, he does not have to fight so continuously for attention.

163

When he shoves forward trying to monopolize the scene, we can say more comfortably, "You want me to give you more attention, I know, dear. I can't now. I've got to get the housework done. But later, I'll be all yours. In our time alone."

One question which parents ask is: *"How shall we introduce this time-alone business?"*

For best results, time alone should not be a haphazard getting together. A child should know that he has it coming and that he can count on it. The secure knowledge of this helps in itself. We should, therefore, introduce the time alone by telling a child about it. "From here on out, I'm going to have a special time alone, all for you every day." Or, if every day isn't possible, then at least three times a week. Both labeling the time *"your time alone"* and *sticking to it* have a salutary effect.

Said Ruth's mother to her, "I know I've never seemed to have time for you all alone. But I'm going to now. Every day, Ruth. You're going to have half an hour all to yourself with me. It'll be our time alone together. And I shan't let anything interfere. . . ."

"Not daddy?" querulously, a frown wrinkling Ruth's forehead.

"Not daddy. Our time will be when daddy's at work."

"And on Sunday?"

"We'll ask him if he won't read the paper and let us have our time."

"Not the telephone?"

"No. I won't go to the phone during our time!"

"But if it rings you'll have to answer."

"No, dear. Not during our time alone."

Ruth relaxed, the wrinkles suddenly gone. This was something new and different. Ruth was important enough to mother so that nothing would stand in the way of her special time. This was strengthening and good.

Six-year-old Kim was not so readily convinced. "I don't believe it," he countered. "It'll be like always. We start to play a game of tick-tack-toe and the phone rings and then you blah-blah-blah for two hours or more."

But gradually Kim saw that his mother meant what she promised. Since this particular block of time was defined as belonging to him, all neatly done up and labeled, he could relax. It was something he had a right to. He didn't have to push and pull and yammer and yell to keep his mother with him. He could settle back, knowing that during a portion of the day at least she would be entirely *his*.

Another question which parents ask is: *"What shall we do with a child in his time alone?"*

We have three jobs to do in our time alone if it is to prove most valuable in preventing and reducing disciplinary ills. Our first job is to let a child know that he can use the time as he wishes. The second job is to help him know that this is a time for intimate sharing. And the third is to help him use at least a part of the time for release of unwanted feelings. The more he can let out the hurts and fears and anger at such times, the less do they need to press at him and burst at other times.

How, then, shall we start time alone?

Let's see what Kim's mother did.

"What'll we do, Mom?" asked Kim after she had told him that they were to have their time alone.

"Anything you like, dear. You be the chooser for now. Perhaps later on I'll have a turn."

Kim nodded. "Let's read," he said, in spite of himself drifting back to accustomed activities wherein mother's focus would be on the book rather than entirely on him.

"Okay," said his mother, because she wanted at first to follow his choice entirely. Later on, if she needed to, she might bring in some suggestions for him to choose from to make the time more intimate and more full of release.

They read that day and the next and the next. And then Kim suggested, "Today I'd just like to sit in your lap."

He sat there, wordlessly, cuddling back against her for the full thirty minutes. He did this for two solid weeks. And then, one day, he sat up beaming and announced, "It's your turn to choose, Mom. What'll it be?"

TIME FOR GETTING "MEAN" FEELINGS OUT

Quickly Kim's mother produced a new box of crayons that she had gotten for just this occasion and a large sheet of drawing paper.

"Suppose you draw a picture and have me just sit here and watch."

But being on the floor and having mother up on a chair did not bespeak as sure a hold on her as sitting in her lap.

"You'll really pay attention?" he asked warily.

"Yes, dear."

"And you won't pick up that knitting?"

"No, dear. I'll just watch."

"Okay," he said with a sigh of relief. "What'll I draw?"

Here was mother's chance. Now, if she said the right thing, she could help Kim to feel free to bring out the feelings that he needed to get rid of, especially the angry feelings that were causing most of their disciplinary fights. So she stopped and thought a moment.

How can I help him get going on bringing his "mean" feelings out?

166

And then she said the wisest possible thing. "You can draw whatever you want, dear. You can draw a mean, ugly, nasty picture if you like. It doesn't have to be a pretty one."

"Real, real mean?"

"Yes."

With a grin, Kim went at it. He drew a horrible, scowling face with a tongue sticking out.

"Now you help, Mom." He handed her a crayon. "You put in the words."

"What words, Kimmie?"

"Make them come from her mouth 'cause she's saying, 'Yah! Yah! Yah! I'm a very mad mother. I'm extra mean.'"

Of his own accord, Kim had made the time one of intimate sharing. His mother's encouragement had then helped him make it a time for release of feelings that would otherwise have piled up and made for disciplinary scenes.

With our own children we may need to do more introducing or defining of both the intimacy and the release. As for the intimacy, we may say, "This is our time for secrets!" To introduce the release, we may suggest, "This is a good time for you to tell me, or show me, those mean feelings that everyone has. Those mean feelings that are better not told nor shown in front of grandma or the neighbors . . ." Or, "There are times when you have mean feelings. Lots of times when you feel cross and angry. Everybody has those feelings. Perhaps you'd like to tell me or show me about them. Perhaps you'd like to draw about them; perhaps you'd like to tell me a story about them and have me write them down! * Or perhaps you'd like to talk about how you feel."

Sometimes a child counters, as Irene did. "But I'm not feeling mean now!"

"I know, dear," her mother said encouragingly. "And yet all of us store up mean feelings that need to come out."

---

* See next chapter for more details on the carrying out of these and other activities for release.

"But I don't feel them now, Mom!"

"It's hard to own up to them. . . ." her mother said, mirroring Irene's difficulty in bringing them out. "We don't like to own up to them."

"But I do, Mom. I want to tell you how mad I feel way down inside!"

As in times of stress, when a child gets too rough and becomes hurtful or destructive, limits have to be drawn. "Yes, I did say you could do what you want. And you can do most anything. But not destroy things. And not hurt me. . . ."

"I can't let you kick me. That's something I can't ever let you do. I know, though, you do have mean feelings toward me, so let's get them out some other way . . . How about making a clay mother and 'giving it' to her? How about drawing a mother and doing things to her? Or making up a story about a boy who does to his mother what you'd like to do to me? You can show me in lots of ways or you can tell me about how you feel. . . ."

FATHER COUNTS TOO

When a child is around four or five, he will probably want father, also, to come into the picture. Until nine or ten, both girls and boys will relish times alone with him. From that age on, a father-son time becomes an almost indispensable thing.

But, for the most profound and most worth-while contact, the usual doings with father need to be revised. Chief to be discarded is the electric-train type of time where son leans painfully on his elbows or fidgets from foot to foot while father has all the fun. Next in line for omission is the toughening-up kind of time where father shows off what a big he-man he is and tries to make son just as big and tough. "Come on, take it like a man, guy. Don't be a sissy; that was just a little sock." The odds are too uneven for contests between a father and child in terms of any physical prowess. Instead of con-

168

tests, frank leadership on father's part is better by far. "Here's how you throw a ball. Here's how you catch one!" But we aren't so concerned with such times here, except to point out that they may call for re-evaluation.

Children need intimate, releasing times with their fathers just as they do with their mothers.

"Please, Daddy," begs five-year-old Patsy, "send mother out to get some cigarettes."

"We've got some, darling."

"Send her out to get some candy."

"We've got some candy."

"Well, send her to get some gas."

"But the car doesn't need gas."

"Oh," said Patsy, dejectedly. And then, with face brightening, she said, "Well, send her to get a puppy."

"Why, dear?"

"'Cause then she could keep busy taking the puppy out walking and you and I could have time alone."

So time alone was inaugurated every Saturday afternoon and Sunday. Patsy promptly changed the label from "time alone with daddy" to "my daddy's time with me." In these times she took her father walking, sang songs with him, asked him to read. One day she approached with an especially bright twinkle in her eye.

"You said we could do anything I want, Daddy?"

"'Most anything, yes!"

"Then, I tell you what!" and her voice went to a whisper. "Today you be my mammy!"

Then with daddy as mammy, she requested that he comb her hair, that he wash her face, that he brush her shoes and, last but not least, that he sew a button on her dress.

But the favorite game of all in their time alone was kick-ball. "Now you kick it to me, Daddy . . . Now I kick it to you." Only, one evening Patsy's father noted that the words

169

were curiously changed. "Now you kick *her* to me, Daddy. Now I kick her to you . . . Kick her hard, Daddy. Kick her real, real hard."

After each kick, Patsy would go into gales of laughter. "That's what she deserved, Daddy. She got it good, that time. That's what she deserved."

Father laughed with her, wondering what she meant and mirroring her feelings. "You want her to get what she deserves."

"Uh-huh," she agreed with a ripple of satisfaction. "She's a naughty mammy and she deserves what she deserves!"

Confessed Patsy's father to her mother later after Patsy had gone to bed, "I didn't know whether I should be party to kicking you around the block or whether I should have taken Patsy to task with a sermon on how grateful she should be to have a mother like you. But I remembered all the stuff you've been telling me. I let her go on and accepted and said back her feelings. I must admit, though, that I did have qualms until I noticed how much sweeter she was to you than she'd been in ages. I guess kicking you around that way helped her to get the bad feelings out . . ."

"And," added Patsy's mother, "that in turn helped to make room for the good feelings to come in."

TIME FOR TALK

Whereas younger children play out their feelings more readily, older children may prefer to talk them out. They, too, need time in which they can be our main concern. They, too, need time in which they can safely bring out their fears and hurts and anger and in which they can spill to us whatever they feel is wrong.

Essentially, the establishment of such a time is the same as for younger children, except that a more flexible sort of arrangement will be in order—a kind of availability rather than a fixed time.

170

fused and more fearful, left alone with a problem that was too heavy for her to handle by herself.

After children have gotten the hang of outspoken feelings, part of the time for talk can become a family affair.

"Look," said Beth and Clay's mother one evening. "I want to let down my hair about this before-dinner mess. By the time I've put the food on the table, I'm worn to a frazzle. Let's sit down and talk. I want to say how I feel and I imagine the rest of you do too."

"Okay," said father. "Shoot."

"Well, here I am stirring up dinner for you people. But do you realize I'm busy? No. In you trot, Beth. 'How do I look, Mother? Is the length of my dress right? Have I got too much lip stick?' . . . Then bang goes the door and in you tear, Clay, and invariably tease Beth and dash to the icebox and get right under my feet! . . . And then you arrive, Will, grumbling like thunder because everything isn't ready and sweet and quiet . . . I get so mad I could scream!"

"You get mad at us all," nods father, acceptant.

"I get mad, too," puts in Clay, morosely defiant. "I'm hungry when I come in and nobody seems to care. . . ."

"You're hungry!" with a snort from Beth. "You're a pig. You can't even wait two minutes for dinner. If you'd stay out of the kitchen, maybe mother could get things done."

"I'm hungry, too," from father. "And tired. I've had a long day in the office and a long ride home and I get in the door and nobody seems to notice me. The most I get is an absent-minded peck."

"Oh Daddy! You're silly! The trouble with you is, you want everybody's attention . . . Nobody has any for me."

"You're a hog!" from Clay.

"We're all mad as can be at each other. . . ." said mother.

"We sure are," added Clay with a chuckle.

"Except me. I'm justified!" said Beth.

"You sweet little angel. . . ."

172

"Gee, Mother!" said sixteen-year-old Allison grumpily. "We never have time to talk."

With a half-attentive grunt, Allison's mother answered equally grumpily, "Well, what have you got on your mind?" And then all at once she stopped in her tracks. *Perhaps there is something to that business I was reading about,* she thought. *I've got to make time for Allison and right now!* . . . So, she put down her book and took off her glasses. "I'm sorry, Allie. I've been a brute, never making time for you. I promise I'll do better from here on out."

"That's swell of you, Mother. Now I feel more like telling you. Gee, I've been wanting to so badly. I need your advice. I think I'm pregnant. . . ."

Allison's mother held on tight to the chair arms. "You think you're pregnant!" She was trying hard to remain acceptant instead of railing and ranting and taking this troubled girl to task in a way that would isolate her and leave her alone with her troubles and make them far worse.

"Oh Mother . . . I've needed so badly to talk." And then the whole pathetic story came tumbling. Still in this age of sophisticated youth, in spite of her own apparent sophistication, Allison had gotten all sorts of erroneous ideas. She had been believing that pregnancy could come by way of the tentative explorations which had transpired with her boy friend. Actually nothing had transpired which could make her pregnant, but the apprehension based on faulty knowledge was still there. Now, through the intimate times of talking which became available, Allison was able to get out her fears, her doubts, her wonderings and to revise and re-evaluate her own desires and attitudes until they were welded into new moralities and new strengths.

Had her mother brushed her off, had her mother not had time to see her alone or had she condemned her when she began getting her fears off her chest, these things would not have happened. Allison would have only grown more co

"I never feel wrong; just wronged. . . ." said Beth again, with a sheepish smile.

Through it all, father and mother have done no censoring. Each person has said what he felt. Neither have father and mother struggled with precepts or rules for solution. Each has brought out his gripes and has listened to the gripes of each of the others. True! Father and mother have condemned certain actions, but they have respected the feelings that each person expressed. Both held the conviction that getting the angry feelings out in the open would of itself bring some solution since, in addition to airing their own feelings, they were also able to accept the others'.

They were right. The before-dinner strain in their family dwindled markedly after three or four times of talk.

"I don't know if it's because each of us is trying to do better of our own will and accord," father tried to analyze what happened. "I don't know if it's because we see each other's point of view better. Or if it's because we all let our feelings out. Whatever it is, it worked. Not one hundred per cent but enough so there's more sense of peace. . . ."

A few nights later his opinion was confirmed. Quite a different kind of talk came into another family conference. This time Clay inaugurated it. "Say," he said, addressing his father and mother, "I need to talk something over with you."

"Me too?" asked Beth, uncertain but eager.

"I guess," said Clay with a touch of the old animosity.

"Clay's not sure he wants Beth," reflected mother, "and Beth wants to stay but isn't sure she should."

"Oh well, let's let her." Clay waved her in with a magnanimous gesture. Then he turned to mother and added, "You made me say it. Perhaps now you're satisfied."

"You feel I made you."

"No," said Clay with a small, wise grin, "I guess I made myself. . . . But it doesn't matter. I've got more important business."

"Let's have it," said father.

"Well, I only have twenty-five cents saved and there's a dog that four of us kids want to buy and I need a dollar more and I wondered if I did a job for any of you if you'd pay me in advance."

"You can make that box for me that I'm supposed to do for shop," said Beth, "and I'll pay you eight cents. That's all the extra I have."

They went on talking, figuring out what Clay could do.

It was mother who finally thought to ask, "What kind of a dog, Clay?"

"It's a Dachspeke."

Beth looked puzzled. "A Chestpeke, you mean?"

"Oh, a Chesapeake," said father.

"No," answered Clay. "It's a new kind of dog. A Dachspeke, with a stomach like a Dachs and ears like a Pekinese."

Suddenly an idea burst from Beth. "Let's canvas the neighbors and see how many will let us mow their lawns."

"Swell!" said Clay. "Will you lend us the lawn mower, Dad?" And from there on they worked as smoothly as any team.

"It never happened before," said mother to father later after the children had gone to bed.

"Not so long ago they would have spent their time seeing who could down the other most effectively."

"But evidently the airing of the meaner feelings that went on last week cleared the air for the sharing that took place today."

PARENTS ALSO NEED TIME ALONE

When parents are in the habit of having time alone with a child, the child in turn grows more content with letting them have time alone together.

"Come on, Buzz," says eight-year-old Cathy to her younger

174

brother. "Can't you see mother and daddy want *their* time alone now."

Respect grows also for time that a parent wants alone by himself. "What are you doing?" asks Roger, eleven, staring down at his mother's perplexed doodlings.

"I need this time, Roger, to figure out some problems that have been on my mind!"

"Oh," murmured Roger with sudden wisdom, "this is your time alone so you can talk to yourself!" And with a look of complete understanding, he went quietly out.

When a child has had time alone with us consistently in his younger years, the sharing and talking things through comes more readily as he grows older.* Although the specific designation of "time alone" will have vanished, the sense of his parents' accessibility and of his own accord with them will persist.

All along, the main thing that counts is our own deep feeling of loving acceptance. This is what gives time alone together a value beyond the sum of the minutes which have transpired. This is the base and the essence that make possible the sharing, the intimacy and the release.

* Further activities that can be used in time alone are described in ensuing chapters.

11. Story books of their own

Nancy, four and a half, sits at the table turning up her nose at the cocoa in front of her, which she had asked for in preference to milk. She is muttering to herself and to the world all at one time. If someone listens, all right. If no one listens, all right too. She will still mutter. Through her muttering at this moment she is getting out feelings of irritation that she has fortunately not been taught to hold in. Her talk comes out rhythmically in a kind of poetry, without rhyme but with much reason.

> I don't like skin on milk,
> Or skin on custard pudding.
> I don't like skin on cocoa.
> I don't like skin.
> Except just skin on me
> Where skin ought to be.

Her mother sits listening, her pencil moving quietly over the sheet of paper. She says nothing; just listens until the chant is over. And then, she nods and acceptantly answers, "You don't like lots of things!"

"No, I don't!" Nancy admits with a smile, gulping the cocoa down.

Again, release and the acceptance and mirroring of feelings has worked.

On another day, in another place, another mother and child are together. They are having their "time alone." Outside, the thunder has been booming its loud way over the house and is now fading off in the distance.

Carl, three, is playing on the floor. He has asked his mother if she would sit in the big chair and watch him build blocks.

Daughter, pensively: "I wrote this one for you."
Father, reading:
"Why does grown-ups' crossness hurt children
Much more
Than children's crossness hurts grown-ups?"

All at once, with a clap of thunder just past, he looks up and says,

The noise—
Up in the sky.
You can't see it.
You can't get it out with a big truck.
It goes under a tree like an airplane.
It didn't come down . . .
But it will *some* day
And then—
It will yell at you
Like you yell at me:
'You bad,
Ugly mommie.'

177

"You'd like it to come down and call me a bad, ugly mommie!"

"Uh-huh!"

"You'd like it to yell at me as I yell at you!"

"Uh-huh!" Carl agreed comfortably, with an air of sharing.

When children are very young, they talk as accompaniment to a great many activities. Without any awareness or effort on their part, their words and phrases fall into rhythmic patterns which are, in effect, small stories or poems. As parents become attuned, they can often hear these poems and capture them by putting them down on paper.

"What are you writing?" asked Sandy, four.

"I'm writing down the mean feelings you were just talking about."

"Read 'em!" Sandy said in a commanding voice, quite hostile.

"You made a poem when you said those mean feelings!"

"Read it!" he said imperiously. "Read the mean poem!"

"You said,

> You make me do things
> I don't want to do.
> I hate to do things.
> I hate you."

"Read it again," he said with a wide grin. "And again," he insisted, climbing up into mother's lap and leaning back against her. "And again!"

Fifteen times he would have it. Then after a great hug, he jumped down and ran off, chanting,

> You make me do things
> I don't want to do.
> I hate to do things.
> I hate you.

"Fine song," said Sandy's father later. "What will the neighbors say?"

"Let's not worry too much about the neighbors. If they can understand, they will; otherwise, they'll talk no matter what we do with Sandy. What's far more important is that I haven't had as peaceful and happy a day since I can remember. It apparently works, this business of children's getting their feelings out and our accepting them."

Meanwhile Sandy's parents had discovered as have other parents that

> READING BACK may serve as a way of
> SAYING BACK what a child feels.

Sometimes a child's words fall into story form rather than into the more rhythmic verse form. Such was Cynthia's monologue to her doll. "I don't like you, you old sniffy face. I'll knock you over. And I'll walk in the mud and I'll walk over you and you'll be a muddy old sniffy face, you will! My shoes will get you all muddy." . . . The form is not of major importance. It's the release that counts.

"Once there was a girl who had to go to the hospital," began Cornelia. "Her mother didn't tell her no lies but the stupid nurse said, 'It won't hurt, dear!' Only it did. She couldn't breathe and bombers and birds flew around and around in a hum and a roar. And she tried to yell and she couldn't. She tried to kick and couldn't. There was only the war."

Cornelia went on and on, her fear working out through her story. Her mother listened, knowing tenderly that draining the fear was the important thing.

MAKING "MEAN" STORIES

With younger children the listening ear can often catch words which inadvertently form little stories. As children

179

grow older, they will often be intrigued with the idea of dictating stories and later of writing or typing them. Many times all they need as a starter for the "release" kind of story is the knowledge that they *may* tell of unhappy and scary and mean things as well as the nice ones. "Your story doesn't have to be about nice things. I can be about things that aren't nice. It can be about the mean things you think about or feel. I won't scold or blame you."

"But you'll lecture me," put in seven-year-old Joan suspiciously.

"I know you feel that way. But truly I won't. You can make your story about anything you wish!"

"About anything?"

"About anything!"

"Even if it's naughty?" she persisted in the usual way of needing reassurance when parents—or teachers—first permit children to bring the hitherto forbidden feelings into view.

"Yes, Joan," guaranteed Joan's mother. "Even if your story is very, very naughty, I won't scold."

"But you've always been scoldy."

"I know I have been up to now. But now I've learned better. I've learned that it helps people a lot to tell about the mean ways they feel."

So Joan started, pausing after the first word and then moving smoothly and rhythmically forward.

> Yesterday—
> I lifted seven flower pots.
> I put them in my tent
> And found they were
> Full of big, bad bugs
> To bite the baby.

Joan's mother nodded. "You wanted them to hurt her!"

"I wanted them to bite her hard and make great big red

bites swell up all over her so she'd be as swelled up as a big red balloon and nobody'd say, 'What a sweet, pretty baby!'"

Joan gave a deep sigh of relief.

"It feels good to be telling me. It's good to get those mean feelings out in words!"

"Yes," said Joan, adding wisely, "and not out in bitings or hittings."

Joan's mother reported two months later. "Joan's been a different child since she's been getting her mean feelings out in all sorts of ways including telling stories. But it didn't happen all at once. At first, she was meaner to the baby. I had to watch every minute. Now she's ever so much friendlier, though, and we have far fewer scenes."

Sarah, ten, was a sensitive child who had frequent asthmatic attacks. She was an extraordinarily good child. "She's never angry," her mother avowed in a group of mothers one day. "In fact, she's so sweet I don't see how I ever get cross at her. I do though, I guess, because I'm so worn out with the housework and stuff. When you say all children have resentful and angry feelings I can't help feeling that Sarah's an exception. I know she hasn't."

However, when Sarah's mother began to understand that emotional troubles could come out in bodily troubles, she inaugurated a time alone with Sarah every day. "After all, if there's even one slim chance that this can help reduce her asthma, I'm for it!" So she assured Sarah that she could tell her, or show her, about all the unhappy and troubled and mean feelings she could think of.

At first Sarah denied having any such feelings. "I don't have, Mother. Honestly, I don't."

"You don't like to remember them, I know. Like me. I don't like to remember about getting cross at you. It makes me so ashamed."

Sarah looked at her mother in surprise. This was the strangest confession she had ever heard. She'd never suspected that

181

her mother had any such sense of shame. Much less had she ever thought to hear about it.

"I go to that group, you know," her mother went on, "and I've learned there that if I get my bothered feelings out in writing I'm not so apt to let them come out on you. So I'm doing it. Want to hear one of the stories I made?"

Sarah nodded.

"Okay, here goes."

> I get so mad working all day long I feel like fury. I have too much to do. The house is too big. The wash is too heavy. The pots and pans and dishes and arguings get in my hair. I'd like to lump it all. I'd like to go on a kicking, tearing, screaming tantrum and throw the washing machine out the window and the carpet sweeper and every dustcloth and broom and choke all the arguers and let the whole place go to pot. . . .

Sarah chuckled appreciatively. "Then we'd live in a pig-sty. But that wouldn't matter, Mom. I know how you feel."

Sarah's mother gulped down the rising tears. Sarah understood her mother better than she had understood Sarah. Here was a child, mirroring feelings, accepting them, instinctively doing the very thing her mother was trying so hard to do.

Then she noticed that Sarah was talking, half as if to her mother, half as if to herself. "Well, I guess if you can do it so can I."

She left the room and her mother heard her clicking away on the old portable in the study. On Sarah's return she brought to her mother a story-poem about one of the small experiences in the daily round of living into which she had apparently been putting the feelings of unsurmountable difficulties which are common on occasion to us all.

"It's about when you're angry at me," said Sarah, shyly handing her mother the sheet.

182

When you're angry—
And I'm making my bed
Everything's a mess.
All the bumps seem bigger;
All the wrinkles seem deeper.
The tucking is bunched up.
    Nothing is right.

I get rough inside also,
And choky.
And I go to bed
And I cough and cough.

"Suddenly it came clear," said Sarah's mother to her father later. "At least a part of her asthma attacks must come as result of her held-in feelings choking to get out."

Sarah's parents were not content, however, to stop here. They took Sarah for professional help. For two years psychological treatment proceeded along with medical treatment. At the same time, Sarah's parents turned increased attention to satisfying Sarah's emotional needs and they continued to accept her feelings, encouraging her to bring them out. Among other things, Sarah kept on writing poems and stories. These she gathered into a loose-leafed binder until it had become quite a sizable book.

In their times alone, Sarah on occasion would turn back the pages. "Remember, Mother, this was the way I felt then?" . . . "Remember when you'd gotten so mad, how afraid I was? But I'm not afraid anymore."

"Not afraid to be mad on your own either."

"No, Mom. Not a bit. It makes us so much better friends."

BOUND BUT FREE

Here are a group of children in fourth grade sitting enthralled, listening to their teacher reading aloud. She is not, however, reading from the printed page. The book she holds is not bound in buckram. It is a loose-leafed binder, covered with gay chintz and divided into different sections, each section marked by means of a sturdy tab with a child's name—Amy, Al, Andy, Barbara, Betty and so on down the line.

"Read us a poem Barbara made," requests one youngster eagerly.

"All right," says the teacher, locating the proper tab and readily flipping the pages.

"Here's one of Barbara's."

> The waves
> Are crashing
> On the beach . . .
>
> A little boy
> Comes running up
> And dives
> *Looping*
> Like a flying fish.

Appreciative smiles go around the room.
"Now read Wanda's frog one!"
Giggles rise before she starts.

> Frogs in the pond
> Three, four, five—
> All covered with bumps!
> I guess they have hives.

Amid the laughter, one child exclaims, "Frogs have *their* troubles, too!"

"So do we all!" said the teacher.

"Read the one about when Jimmie was afraid of dying and made the engine poem and we talked about how we all wanted to be like that engine and have part of us stay alive for always. . . ."

> Where do old engines go
> When they're finished,
> When they're old,

And new bright shiny engines
Take their places?
What happens to them
When they've grown
Useless
And old?

Can't part of them
Keep living
In the new ones,
In the young ones?
Can't they give
Just a whistle or a smokestack,
Just a piston or cow-catcher
To the new ones?
And that way
Stay,
And not go
Altogether.

"Now read a mean one. The new one I made today."

"All right!" the teacher said, locating it quickly. "Bill called this new one, 'The Wicked Man.' "

Do you know who the wicked man is? I know but I won't tell. He looks like a guy named Bill. He's very wicked. He doesn't like anybody. And he can do what he wants to them because he's very big. He's a giant. He says to his father and mother, "Lie down," and they have to because he's so big and they're scared of him. "Yes, Bill," they say. "Yes, Bill. All right, Bill. Yes, Bill. Yes."

So they lie down and he steps all over them with his big feet. He kicks them and steps on them and they cry and cry and beg for murcy. So he finely gives in in case they'll promise always to be good.

And so it goes on, the reading back of children's thoughts and feelings—feelings of anger and hurt and apprehension and feelings, too, about the droll whimsies and the flashes of beauty that come into view.

It had started by the teacher's saying, "You can write stories or poems about anything you wish and we'll put them into a *book of your own*. You can write about nice feelings or mean feelings, about any kind you want. You can write them down yourselves or dictate them to me, whichever you prefer."

She had gone on to let them know that all people have mean feelings and that these are better out on paper than out in episodes of hair pulling and window smashing.

For a while, the class responded in what to them was both intriguing and bad. They went wild in an orgy of obscenity. Every other word was a four-letter monosyllable. "I'd no idea there were so many! But I kept on trying to get the feelings that were coming out. I kept on reflecting, 'You feel that's very bad!'

"The second phase was a deluge of murder with every known weapon, in every known way. But, gradually, this seemed to have played itself out and more and more lovely bits began to come in." As the teacher commented, "They seemed to be more open to lovely things. I guess, as always, the positive feelings do have more space to enter when the troubled ones have been at least somewhat cleared out." *

At home, parents can also make books of a child's own poems. Into either a plain or covered binder can go the gay, the lovely and the unlovely and troubled feelings, all of which might otherwise have stayed shut inside a child's mind.

The most important things in connection with the writing of poems are these: Your interest in him; real focus on and delight and satisfaction in what he says and feels. Letting him be free in what he says and how he says it. Not making his poems rhyme. They don't have to. A lot of verse by the best of our poets doesn't. Encouraging him to be himself. And, as always, accepting whatever comes.

Barbie, six, dictates, and her mother feels the little hairs rise on the back of her neck at the beauty and accuracy of Barbie's descriptions.

* See also Chapter 14 for what teachers have done and can do in schools.

186

Birds fly like waves.
Birds fly like water from icicles
Falling straight down.
Birds fly as if
They were dancing on air.

She reads back Barbie's poem and Barbie's dreamy look matches her own. At this moment Barbie and her mother are not only parent and child. They are two people who together are relishing something good.

"I've got a new story in my mind to put in my book," announced another six-year-old. Diana's eyes are alight with mischief. "It's about being naughty."

"All ready," said mother, taking pencil in hand.

I didn't come when you called.
I just sat on the grass,
The sun shining on me.
I sat there till I was too hot—
I was too hot to move,
I was too hot to do anything.
I couldn't come.
I couldn't move.
I couldn't do anything.
And so—
I just stayed there
Till you stopped calling
And the sun
Went away.

Harriet, twelve, has written of her fears and now comes to her mother and thrusts the book of her own stories into her mother's hands. "I couldn't quite tell you, Mother, but I wrote it. It's been bothering me so."

I'm afraid to go out with my stepfather. He gets so mad at everything. I pick up my fork and he says, 'Don't do it that way, do it this way.' I get to feeling as if I had thimbles on every one of my fingers and as if I can't do a damn thing right.

187

"It makes you feel terrible," Harriet's mother accepted Harriet's feelings instead of scolding or trying to defend her new husband's position. Inside of her she wondered, *Is this part of the reason why Harriet has been so stand-offish to me and so unfriendly?* But her thoughts got no further for suddenly Harriet's arms were around her.

"Oh, Mother. I'm so glad you understand!"

Harriet had once more demonstrated the all-important fact: As children talk and write out their feelings and as parents accept and say or read these back, not only do the disciplinary ills diminish but new relationships and understandings occur.

12. Mudpies and rainbows

Ages back, in the shadows of time, primitive man used pictures on the walls of his caves as a means of communication. Today man still uses pictures but for another purpose: to express the more primitive impulses in him. Both adults and children can sometimes paint out feelings more readily than they can talk them out. At times a picture can be more expressive than words. A picture can serve as an impetus which starts off the translation of feelings into words.

Marvin is a lanky, too-thin sixteen-year-old, painfully shy. "He's a good kid," says his father, "if only he'd come out of himself a bit and show more gumption. He holds back all the time as if he's scared something will happen if he opens his mouth."

With Marvin's very first painting his father came upon a clue as to what lay behind the boy's shyness. The drawing itself, done in colored chalks, was sketchy and crude, but it possessed the kind of authenticity that comes when a person paints with the strength of his feelings prompting him. In it were three figures simply placed on the sheet without interference of background details. An angel with a harp ascending heavenward. A pugilist with bulging biceps. And a lanky, blank-faced lad with droopy mouth.

189

"Like to tell me about it?" his father asked Marvin.

"I guess!" Marvin said half-heartedly, "if you're sure you meant what you said when you promised you wouldn't get mad no matter what I drew."

"I meant it."

"I should be treated like a man now. But this is how they make me feel."

"Well," he went on, with an unwonted smile, "this one here" —the angel—"that's me like you and mother want me to be! . . . This one here"—the boxer—"that's how I'd like to be! But here, this one—the dope—that's how I am."

Marvin's father had been right in surmising that fear lay behind the boy's shyness. It was a fear of not being able to live up to what was expected of him. The drawing had brought this out.

"It started us on a new path," reported Marvin's father.

"It made me see, fast, just like that, where I'd been off the track!"

Gloria was a seventeen-year-old who was getting into constant scrapes. "As if she were trying deliberately to give us gray hairs and shorten our lives," stated her mother. Gloria's pictures were without any definite form, masses and streaks of color. One done in reds Gloria described as "the sunset's anger at having to keep the world warm!" A series of crisscross lines done in black and gray she called "The Prison Window!" Another in streaks of dirty brown she labeled, "The Witches' Brew," and commented, "The witch drank it by mistake and fell down dead." As Gloria continued, it became apparent that the sun's anger was Gloria's own, that the prison was the prison that held her, while the witch was essentially her mother whom she often wished dead. "But I wished her dead far less often," said Gloria as postscript several months later, "after I'd gotten my feelings out onto paper!"

In some homes, the grownups as well as the children use paints as a means of getting out feelings. "We have a painting group a couple of evenings a week," one father recounted, "just the four of us, my wife, the two children and myself. I started it off by saying, 'We're not going to try for finished productions—not in this painting class. We don't care whether a cat looks like a cat or a calf. We don't care whether we paint things in their real color or use a pretend color instead. We don't care how crazy the drawing is. What we do care about is painting the way we feel. We're going to make pictures of how we feel when we're hurt or scared and pictures about how we feel and what we'd like to do when we're mean and mad . . . Pictures about when we've been embarrassed or when we've wanted something we couldn't get, or about things we had to do but didn't want to . . . You know, that sort of picture!'"

Like a flash six-year-old Marilyn got the idea. "Let's draw about people we don't like," she cried in shrill excitement.

191

"Let's draw about people *here* whom we don't like!" shouted eight-year-old Vance, going Marilyn one better.

"You mean what we seem like to each other when we don't like each other?"

"Uh-huh."

So mother drew a sketch of children who ran the other way when their mother called them to dinner. Father painted about mother when she ironed his shirts too stiff. Vance's picture was of a girl, strangely marked like a peppermint stick with diagonal red stripes from head to toe. "That's Marilyn when you guys think she's sweet as sugar!" But it was Marilyn who worked longest and hardest and had the most to say. She made a room with a desk containing writing materials and a table all set for lunch and, in the room, a woman with a black face. "Black because she's mad. . . ."

> She's cross and angry—
> So angry she can't eat her lunch
> The coffee's in the pitcher,
> The coffee's in the pot.
>
> And the desk is sitting
> All ready for her
> With the ink on it
> For her to write with;
> And her hair all up in a bun,
> And heels on her feet.
>
> She's busy now.
> She's very busy.
> She's writing with her ink pad.
> She's doing it fast.
> She sat down with a *bump*.

"She always sits down hard when she gets mad," added Vance appreciatively, his resentment toward his mother making him join the enemy camp.

"Then you both feel mad at her for getting mad!" their father said, mirroring their feelings.

192

They went on letting out resentments against each other, finding each other strangely acceptant—something that had never happened before.

"But you should have seen them an hour later," their mother said, reviewing what had happened. "I don't believe we've had as peaceful and as cooperative a time getting ready for bed in all our lives."

An investment in supplies for painting out feelings proves its own worth within a very short time. There are several kinds of things one can get. Poster paints and large brushes. Crayons in gay, spectrum hues. Chalks that look like the sticks used on school blackboards, but vivid in color and soft in quality. These are among the most useful. Sheets of paper not less than twelve by eighteen. Loads of newspapers spread on the kitchen floor and table or wherever no one will mind the mess. And, if it's soft, powdery chalk that one is drawing with, then also some clear lacquer to spray on with an insect spray to "fix" the colors and keep them from smudging off.

USING HANDS INSTEAD OF FISTS

Another good medium is finger paints. These can be bought all ready mixed. A glazed paper comes with them which is spread flat and wet down before one begins to paint. But there is no brush. Fingers and hands, even arms and elbows, are used instead.

"It works so smoothly," purrs Angela, thirteen, making swirls and whirls and curlicues with her fingers and the sides of her hands. And then her expression changes. She flattens the paint's surface and commences drawing with more defined purpose. She draws a boat, rocking on a deep blue ocean against a deep blue sky. A figure is leaning over the side of the boat, obviously in the grip of seasickness. "That's how I'd like her to get griped when she gripes me!" announces Angela, clenching her teeth.

"You feel mighty angry," reflects Angela's mother.

193

"I sure do, when you get angry at me."

"And you'd like to see me suffer." Angela's mother goes on mirroring what Angela's picture has shown. She says this with loving acceptance, without blame or condemnation, knowing that when enough of Angela's resentment has come out and has been received with understanding, far friendlier feelings will come into play.

Four-year-old May reacts in a typical small-child way to the slippery feel of the finger paints. "It's squishy," she shrieks. "It's gooshy. . . . It's bee-emmy goosh. . . ." As she smears in it, she apparently plays out some of the resentment against the too severe toilet training her parents had imposed on her earlier before her mind and muscles were ready. In her painting, she uses the stuff representing the "dirt" from her own body to "do dirt" to others. "I'll smear her up. . . ." she crows. "I'll smear her up good."

As we've seen in an earlier chapter, a child often thinks of the products of elimination as a weapon. Then, as he goes on living, anything that symbolizes these products becomes a kind of symbolic weapon. From small children to grown men we use words of defecation to deprecate and smear the enemy. It is only a short jump from a child's "old doo-doo!" to an exclamation not uncommon in adult usage, containing a four-letter word which means the same thing. Because the impulse is so widespread, we won't be surprised to see our own children turning to gleeful smearing as a way of eliminating the "nastiness" they feel.

When children paint or draw out feelings there are several pointers that we will want to keep in mind if the disciplinary tensions are to be eased.

Don't interpret a picture for a child. Let him tell you about it and keep on mirroring his feelings.

Don't put any emphasis on the way he draws things. Perspective, proportions and the like have no place in this kind of painting.

Don't say, "That looks more like a helicopter than a spider." If he feels it's a spider—that's what counts.

Give a child space and colors and paper and the signal to go ahead. . . .

If you wish, tell him his feelings are often strange and unformed. "You only half-know what they are." Well, his paintings may turn out that way too.

Best of all, try painting out feelings yourself. . . .

"But I can't paint!" you protest. "I've never learned to draw."

One does not need to learn. To feel and explore—these are far more important. "*Be* angry!" . . . "*Be* hurt!" . . . "*Be* full of the feeling, whatever it is and let your hands spontaneously do the rest."

FIGURES OF EARTH

Clay is another medium through which children can get out their feelings. There are two kinds of clay: "oily clay" and "watery clay" as one child called them. The oily clay is of the plasticine type. It doesn't harden or dry out. The watery clay is potter's clay. With water added, it becomes as "gooey" and "guishy" and "sticky" as mud on a rainy day. With the water dried out, it "turns into statues," it becomes "hard as a rock or as elephants' teeth."

Both the oily clay and the watery clay are useful. Small children ordinarily prefer the latter. If kept at the right consistency by having it "just wet enough," it is more easily malleable than the oily type. "It doesn't have to be held all day till your hand makes it warm enough to squish."

Often small children identify the clay with bodily products. One youngster makes small rolls of clay, a flock of them, and says, "They're worms come to eat you! They're b.m. bombs out of the toilet to smear you up!"

Sometimes a child gets out a lot of the "nastiness" in him through the messing itself. He says nothing to identify the clay with elimination but he obviously enjoys the stickiness and wetness. He smears in it as if it were the most glorious thing. In contrast, a child may be afraid of putting even the tips of his fingers into the clay. Una, three, shows quite clearly why.

Mother: "Come on now, Honey."
Honey: "But it's not my turn to be clean yet."

Una is a sullen, unsmiling baby who stutters almost as if she were afraid to bring out the words. When she first saw clay, she touched it tentatively and drew back as though she had been bitten. "Bad girl!" she scolded herself, stuttering painfully. "Don't you touch that potty stuff."

Una had been prodded earlier about many things. She had been strictly scheduled, strictly weaned, strictly cleaned. She had never been allowed to bring out her anger. In fact, she had been severely scolded whenever she was cross. The clay now represented potty stuff to her and potty stuff anywhere but in the potty stood for being naughty. She wanted to be naughty, as her subsequent behavior showed. She wanted to smear the clay over everything as an aggressive, hostile act. She did this later, reveling in it. But at this point now she was too afraid.

As she drew back, the nursery-school teacher reflected her feelings. "Una, you don't want to touch the clay!"

"Not touch. Dirty. Bad."

Gradually, however, Una came to use the clay along with other materials to release her aggression. And as it drained, her stutter decreased.

Wally, also three, takes the clay and brings out his angry feelings in more direct fashion. "Make Buzz," he directed his mother, handing her a hunk of clay. So she threw together a rough figure to represent his brother, so crude that she had it done in two minutes. Then, painstakingly, Wally rolled tiny sausagelike bits and stuck them all over the clay effigy. "I'm putting ickies on him cause he busted my bucket . . ."

To herself his mother wondered, *His bucket? What on earth does he mean? His bucket is still right over there in the sandbox as whole as can be.* Aloud, she did no more then repeat his words, being unsure of his intent. "You want to put ickies on him because he busted your bucket."

"Uh-huh," he said, with a mad look. "He busted it here." And he clutched his buttocks in a telling gesture.

"You mean he busted your buttocks?"

"Uh-huh, he busted my bucket. He kicked me, that's what he did."

Children use clay in many other ways. Sam, seven, was particularly violent. He made a clay effigy—a "big man— eight, nine, ten feet tall. He's got a mustache like my father," he said, giving the man's identity. Then he launched into a diatribe. "I'll stick him in the stomach and burst him open. I'll slit him with a knife and kill him with a rake and make him *absolutely* dead."

"Believe you me I was shocked," confided Sam's mother.

197

"I'd seen my husband handle Sam with an iron glove but I'd no idea Sam's hostility was so violent. It showed us a thing or two, and his father caught on fast. Sam didn't seem to trust him, however, until after he'd gotten out a lot more of the hostility. Too much of it had apparently been stored up and needed to be released before Sam could accept a new dad. It was only after a lot more had come out—over a period of about eight months I'd say—that things improved. But they're so different now, it was well worth while."

Clay may be bombs "to kill the whole world dead with, especially at a certain address." Clay may be snakes "for to bite you with." Clay may be "dirty worms to crawl over you and make you itch." Clay may become a "man to stamp on" or a "mother to squeeze the bejuices out of." It may be fashioned into ugly caricatures with big lips or noses, with warts on cheeks or chin. It may become an effigy to "stick full of splinters." Or it may, like eighteen-year-old Victor's leering gargoyle, be a "self-portrait." Says Victor, "It's the killer inside me. It used to jut out over the bed at night and frighten me to death. But it doesn't come around any more now that I've gotten it out into a shape that I can see and touch!"

13. The play's the thing

RADIO RACKETS, MOVIE MURDERS AND KILLER CARTOONS

"My child has murder on the mind. It's because of those horrible radio programs. I know it is!" . . . "It's because of those dreadful funny books that aren't funny at all but full of killer-dillers!" . . . "It's because of those wild and wooly movies that he insists on seeing every blessed week."

The radio programs, the comic books and the wildest of movies are far from desirable. But they are not the *cause* of the aggression in our youngsters. The aggression, as we know by now, is already there. A child feels himself small and weak next to the adults who tower above him. He desires to be greater and bigger—more powerful. He musters aggression to this end. A child feels resentful and angry of many things as he grows. He wants to be able to let out and get even. He wants to bring out the "murderous" impulses that lie within.

In the radio programs to which he listens, in the comics and movies, other characters bring out and express the aggression which he may not. This feels good to him. He gets a vicarious thrill from it. He identifies himself with the characters who are what he is inside and who do what he would like to do.

"When I see one of those killer pictures," said nine-year-old Wallace, gulping down his excitement, "gee, *I* get to be the man with the gun. I never have any other chance."

To Wallace these pictures mirrored feelings which lay in him and for which he had not had enough outlets in the daily course of his life. So also did the comics that he collected and the radio programs to which he clung. Wallace himself was full of aggression that dated back to his earliest years.

"I see it so clearly now," said his mother. "We sat on him too much for the bad things when he was little. We urged him

Father: "Let's get on with the show . . ."
Junior: "Well, I'll tell you . . . If this were a real duel and these were real pistols and we were supposed to count to 10, I would only have counted to 3. . . ."

on too much with the good things. We pushed him into doing more than he could do comfortably. We wanted to show him off in a way that would reflect to our own glory as parents of a prodigy. He resented all this and still does, although *less*, I think, in even the short while since we've been helping him to get his aggression out."

The comics and such appealed to him for one strong reason

above all else: the people in them could be cruel and vindictive for him. They did what he had no way of doing. He got his satisfaction from them by imagining himself in their boots.

Many people believe that children get an outlet for their aggression through such means. Actually, they don't get enough. For people do not adequately release their aggressions through vicarious participation. The passivity of looking on provides none of the *activity* that is needed to reduce hostile feelings. The outlet for aggression remains the shadow rather than the substance. The child identifies with the bad man, the superman, or the good man who shoots straight and true. But all along he is only the onlooker, the stand-in, the double. He is not actually taking part. As a ten-year-old put it, "You know of course that you're not the real McCoy. You like to tell yourself you are but you're always disappointed when you wake up."

The child is not the doer. He is not getting his feelings out through anything *he* himself does. "I just sit and let things run into me off the screen!" says Marianna, describing the passive attitude that prevails. The outlet is secondhand. It's a makeshift for the living stream that stirs and pushes to be actively expressed.

Nor do the killer-dillers suggest any valid channels through which the stream can be diverted. Much of what the majority of comics contain is lurid, sex-laden, and sadistic stuff. Decapitated or armless bodies of beautiful women who have been mutilated. Full-breasted girls being beaten. Sex and hostility all mixed together. These are not any channels for our children to pursue.

Of themselves, the wildest and wooliest, the cruelest and the sexiest of dramas or picture strips will not make our children into delinquents or criminals. But they do present ways of channeling aggression which are unwholesome ways.

We have to offer strong competition by providing ways that are more wholesome—that carry neither threat nor hurt nor

201

harm. For, in general, the child to whom the killer-dillers appeal most is also the child who has the most aggression to be released. It is for this very reason that he so avidly embraces the aggression in what he sees and hears.

Strange as it may seem, it is far more wholesome to draw pictures of mother and call them ugly and horrid. It is far more wholesome to let out all sorts of hateful feelings on what is recognizably mother than to sit and plot and imagine how one can carry out Crime Number Eight on some substitute female. As we know, unless a child lets out on the person who incurs the anger, he may well continue on and on with a string of substitutes all his life.

Being honestly angry and letting the anger come out honestly against the person who has engendered it, yet channeling it into harmless channels—this, as we've seen, does do good. It is the MOST REALISTIC ANTIDOTE for the appeal of the comics and such.

Wallace's parents tried it. They saw to it that he had many of the active outlets we've been talking of all through this book. They found that as he got his "mean feelings" out in the ways that we've been considering, the pull of the comics automatically lessened. The radio programs he had clung to no longer mattered so much. The whole problem fell into proper place even though nothing had been done to forbid or punish or prevent.

Those parents who have tried forbidding as a way of coping with the problem report over and over that it does no good. The child manages somehow to get his fare on the sly. Moreover, the forbidding generates new hostility. The child feels that his parents are cutting off important mutual interests which he shares with "the other kids." He holds this against them and adds it to a score of other injustices he feels. And this in turn feeds into his hostility and makes it grow.

The flank attack is far better: the solution lies in providing other outlets galore. Other outlets that channel aggression and release it more *actively* and more *directly*. And this we are learning to do as we read this book.

ONE CHILD IN HIS TIME PLAYS MANY PARTS

We remember well from our own childhood days how we loved dressing up and playing that we were bigger than we were. We've seen the same sort of enjoyment in our children. A paper crown on the top of a child's head can bring him the dignity of a king, a stick in his hand can give him the courage of a conqueror. With a frayed skirt, a child becomes mother; with a stringy tie, he becomes father.

A chest of scraps and discarded clothing is a storehouse that permits of untold variations in playing things out. This is an old and treasured fact born out by our own memories. There are new facts that can be added today, born out of new psychological knowledge.

"You can be any kind of mother you want," says Elsie's mother. "A mean mother, an angry mother, a cross mother, a nasty mother. Any kind that you like!"

"Oh," says eight-year-old Elsie, who up to this point had been putting on an act with her sister of doing everything nice that a mother does. "Oh," she repeats. "I was waiting till you went out of the room for that part."

"But that's the part I'd like most to see."

"So you can see yourself as others see you!" came the answer quick as a flash.

Elsie's mother had come to understand that acting out was not the whole story if Elsie's disciplinary problems were to be helped. Her own presence was needed. Were Elsie to express her resentment and anger surreptitiously, the fear of these feelings might keep on growing because of the anxiety over possible discovery. This fear might only add to Elsie's inner discomfort, pressure and tenseness. It could augment her dissatisfaction with and her anger at the world. On the other hand, by being present and accepting Elsie's feelings, her mother could help her fear to discharge in ways that would not make it boomerang and increase.

Sometimes family dramas are so simply enacted that no costumes or stage sets or props are needed. "I wish you could see yourself when you get mad," says seventeen-year-old Aileen morosely to her mother.

Says Aileen's mother to herself, *Aileen thinks I'm mad no matter what I say. I used to be mad much oftener, I realize. But since I've developed these new understandings I don't feel mad. And yet, Aileen still carries over her anger against me and reads madness into everything I do. I'm defeated before I start!*

Aloud she says, "You'd like me to see myself mad. Could you show me?"

"How do you mean?"

"Could you show me the way I seem to you . . . Sort of mimic me or act it out? Show me as if you were me? I can be you and we can have a scene where I'm picking on you for something. Let's see! What?"

"When I come in late at night."

"Okay. Here I am . . . No, I mean, here you are coming up the steps. . . ."

"And here you are, calling out, 'Aileen, is that you?' "

Mother as Aileen: "Yes, mother." [And aside] "I wish mother wouldn't always stay awake for me."

Aileen as mother: "Aileen, you're late again. Can't you ever be depended on? You're no infant, you know. My hair's getting gray because of you. And see all these wrinkles? They're your fault; not age, I tell you . . ."

Mother as Aileen: "But mother, none of the other kids have to be in so early and I get furious at you for making me."

Aileen as mother [with an injured air]: "*You* should get furious! *I'm* the one!"

At this point mother intercepts. "Let's change parts. I'll be the mother now and you go back to being Aileen."

Mother as mother [repeating Aileen's last speech]: "*You* should get furious! *I'm* the one!"

Aileen as herself: "Yes, yes! You're always the injured party. How well I know it. And the holier-than-thou attitude you've developed lately is no disguise. It only makes things worse . . . 'Yes, my darling child! *I* understand!' . . . Only you don't . . . Weren't you ever young?'"

For awhile the dialogue goes on with Aileen's getting out a lot of the griping she had not been able to voice before. Then all at once she chuckles. "You know, Mother, we've left out an important character. Dad. Here he is in his bed. I'll be him."

Aileen as father: "Mind your mother, Aileen . . . Snore. Snore. Snore!"

In schools, in youth groups, in parent education classes psychodramas of family life have been readily enacted and have provided release of feelings and growing awareness of each other's needs. In some homes, such an activity may seem artificial. In others, it may appeal, depending on personal preferences. Many children in their teens prefer the more direct approach of talking things over, expressing feelings freely as their parents grant them freedom to do so. Younger children are inclined to dramatize their feelings more eagerly, on the whole.

"How about you boys putting on a radio act for us?" asks the father of Don, seven, and John, nine.

"What about?"

"Well, let's have it about a family like ours. About a mother and father and two boys. It can be a mean act, too. It doesn't have to be all nice. The boys can be as bad as they want. . . ."

Scene 1: Act I

Daughter: "I'm the mother and this is my whip to switch the children." Son: "No, siree. I'm the father and that's *my* privilege."

"How about the parents being mean? Or doesn't that count?" asked John.

"You want it to count."

"Sure I do. Six strikes against them."

Don nodded excitedly. "I do too."

So the two of them crouched beside the radio cabinet under a blanket "so as not to show because it isn't television tonight." And they put on an act in which mother and father were having a fight. "And such language you've never heard," exclaimed their father afterward. "I didn't realize they had either until they were half through."

Puppet plays can also be productive. "I'll clunk you over the head!" says Inez, eleven, making the witch character represent her mother. "I'll clunk you if you do that!" she adds, bringing in a policeman as a kind of father-person, or at least as a higher authority who takes the child's part. But then in the end the child herself vanquishes all by dropping tear bombs down the chimney and making every oldster in the family cry.

Still another activity that has proved of value is a child's concocting comic strips of his own. Through his series of sketches he plays out, step by step, his hurts or resentments or fears. This is what Hermina did. Her drawings were crudely done. They were nothing more than rough little pencil scrawls of a mother and a ten-year-oldish child like herself. The two were sitting at a dinner table, their conversation, done in lettered legends, coming out of their mouths. Hermina brought the strip to her mother and together they read:

PICTURE 1:

> *Mother:* I want more potatoes.
> *Daughter:* There are no more.

PICTURE 2:

> *Mother:* Where are they?
> *Daughter:* In my stomach. . . .

Mother chuckled and said back what Hermina had said, "They're in the girl's stomach. Her mama wants them but she can't get what she wants."

Hermina nodded and returned to the "comic."

PICTURE 3:

> *Mother:* You big pig.
> *Daughter:* Maybe you are. . . .

"She's getting even there, the daughter is," Hermina's mother mirrored Hermina's vengeance and turned back to the cartoons.

PICTURE 4:

> *Mother:* Shut up, you.
> *Daughter:* Maybe I don't have to.

"She doesn't want to give her mother the best of it, does she?"
"No, she doesn't."
"She's mad at her mother."
"You bet she is."

PICTURE 5:

> *Mother:* Shut up or I'll slap you.
> *Daughter:* Oh, yeah.

PICTURE 6:

> *Mother:* You want me to slap you. You are asking for it.
> *Daughter:* Oh, yeah.

Said Hermina's mother, acceptantly, at this point, "The daughter's still got the upper hand. She looks glad."
"But," said Hermina sadly, "it can't last."

PICTURE 7:

> *Mother:* Shut up or I'll slap you.
> *Daughter:* Oh yeah!

But this time the child had a scowl on her face as of gathering tears. And then came the last cartoon in which the mother was beating the daughter with a cane. The daughter was emitting a huge HOW YOW and underneath was the caption, "Nothing's any use!"
For a few moments Hermina's mother was silent while Hermina uncomfortably shifted her weight. To Hermina's
208

mother this was a kind of test. What could she say? Would it help? Could it? It could help only, she knew, if she could feel with her child as Hermina herself had been feeling. Helpless and hopeless. Hurt and fearful that she had no way out. For it was this sort of feeling that came clear now in the crude cartoons.

"I know, darling," said Hermina's mother. "The girl feels quite hopeless. Sort of beaten. . . ."

She felt her child's body on the sofa beside her lean toward her and relax.

"Oh, mother!" said Hermina, her voice scarcely more than a whisper. "But she doesn't feel that way anymore."

THE DO-AS-I-SAY GAME

With younger children a chance to play mother or father and have mother or father take the part of the child has unending appeal.

"Get up. Sit down. Take your shoes off. The other one first, you dumbie. No, the other one," shouts Gus who is five. "Sit on the toilet. No, don't you dare get up. You stay there. You stay there for fifteen hours. No, don't you do that. If you do that I'll make you do something else. Don't you know you never do what you're supposed to do 'cause you're supposed to do it the other way."

"I ask you," groaned Gus's mother. "Is it Gus or is it me?

"But the punch line came at the end when the play was over and Gus turned and questioned sweetly, 'Isn't it hard to be a child and have to take all those orders?' "

Said Gus's mother, "I could have wept."

Fanny, six, requested one day, "Let's play the do-as-I-say game. Let's go to market. Here, I'm the mother and you be the child. This bush is the oranges and this bush is the bananas and these rocks are the nuts. Now, I'm the mama—remember?—and I say, 'Don't you touch those oranges.' Only (in an aside) you go touch them so I can spank you. And the

209

bananas, too. And the nuts and the apples and potatoes. Every single one. You touch every one when I say, 'No.' "

"You want a chance to spank me!" her mother said, mirroring Fanny's feelings.

"Uh-huh, just pretend!"

"But fun to pretend!"

"Uh-huh."

Linton, five, is less obvious in what he does. For about six months his parents had been giving him chances to get out his feelings. When he was mad at the baby he had a baby doll to pound. "You feel mean to the baby, I know. You can't fight with the baby but you can instead with the baby doll. . . ." When he was angry at his mother for her ministrations to his younger brother, he had been given a pillow to let out on. "You can give it to this instead of to me. . . ." But somehow Linton had failed to progress.

Then came an evening after Linton was asleep in his bed when mother and father had gone into one of their violent explosive times together, which they claimed however, Linton never heard. "We never let him see the least bit of dissension. We know, at least, that it isn't *that!* That can't be bothering him. We're terribly careful and never even argue when he's around."

Whether Linton got the general tension in the atmosphere or whether a part of the quarreling reached him in the mysterious terms of being only half heard and not at all seen, they were never to know. All they knew was that the next day Linton enacted a scene.

"Will you come do what I say now?" he asked his mother.

"Yes," she replied.

"You come outside with me," he ordered.

Obediently she followed.

"See!" he pointed up the street to where a workman was noisily drilling through the pavement with a trip hammer.

"Get me one of those things, Mommie."

210

"One of those things, dear?"

"Those noisy bangers."

"What for?" she asked, nonplussed.

"For daddy. Cause then he can get his bad feelings out by banging the street."

"Believe me, that made me see straight," added Linton's mother in the telling. "Our feelings needed as much attention as his. All at once I saw very clearly what the trouble had been. It helps a child to get out his feelings and have them accepted. When enough of the undesirable ones have come out, he's supposed to be calmer and more positive so that discipline grows easier. I'd seen these things. But I'd overlooked another important aspect. You're also supposed to supply him with the fundamental emotional satisfactions he needs. Well, we were attending to one part of the picture but not to the other. We couldn't give him real security and a real sense of belonging in a safe, harmonious home when we ourselves were at such outs."

A year later, however, the picture was different. What with Linton's mother and father attending to their own feelings and continuing to accept his, they had met his needs more soundly. As a result, Linton had correspondingly moved ahead.

PLAYING DOCTOR

When a child has undergone a painful or frightening experience, playing out the hurt and the fear may help to get it off his mind instead of his harboring the shadow of it perhaps for years.

Debby, six, has had her tonsils out. She seemed to come through the experience with flying colors. "It didn't faze her," her mother reported. But one curious and upsetting sequel did occur. Debby began to have nightmares.

"Perhaps she was more afraid than we imagined," her parents were quick to admit.

So, the next afternoon, her mother gave Debby a chance to play out her experience. She started by announcing that Debby's doll needed her tonsils out. "Would you like to be the doctor?"

Debby nodded. "This box will be the wheeling bed."

Then Debby pretended that the bed went up in the elevator "to the highest floor where all the witches were and the ghost-man came like on Hallowe'en only he put a great big flat tire over my nose and blew poison gas into it. . . ."

Over and over again Debby played it, her eyes large and frightened. Her mother *did not try to set her straight by explanations.* She did not try to correct the child's impressions. She did not try to show her that the witches had been nurses and the ghost-man the doctor. She knew that all the rational explanations in the world would not touch Debby's fear. For what Debby felt was based on unreason, not reason, and *the only way to correct it was to let it come out.* Instead she kept saying, "Show me more" . . . "Tell me more." She kept reflecting Debby's feelings of fear and alarm. "The girl was so frightened" . . . "She didn't like it!" . . . "She was mad at the ghost-man for putting the flat tire over her face" . . . Debby's mother geared what she said into what Debby showed of her feelings. All along her efforts were directed at seeing what Debby's feelings were and of understanding, accepting and saying them back.

Debby played the thing out, repetitiously, at least a dozen times. And then, one day the scene changed miraculously.

"The wheeling bed goes up in the elevator and the ladies are there all in white and smiling. They say, 'Little girl, we'll make you all well.' And the doctor comes and says, 'I'm going to make you go round in a ring-around-a-daisy and you'll get sick and then you'll get better and your tonsils will make your throat all sore and you'll get ice cream and no more colds."

"A bit garbled but much straighter than it had been," com-

212

mented Debby's mother as she reported that the nightmares had gone.

A certain wise doctor keeps a small plastic doll in his office dressed in a doctor's white coat. When he has to give a child a "shot" to immunize him, he reflects the child's feelings of hurt and fear and anger and, furthermore, lets the child play out his feelings by giving a shot to the doctor doll. He does not say, "Now, fellow, it didn't hurt." Instead he says, "It didn't feel good" or "It did hurt, I know" or "It made you good and mad to have me stick you. . . ." depending on the child's response.

Child after child plays getting back at the doctor with tears turning into a grin of relief.

There are many frightening things that a small child doesn't quite understand but which his body must undergo in the process of keeping physically well and getting over small or big illnesses. But the fright can be eased and digested as it is played out.

MUTINY IN MONOLOGUE

When children are very little, they themselves often quite spontaneously act out their feelings. Then, as we listen, we can hear many things about ourselves that prove enlightening. And this, too, has value.

Shirley, three, is preening in front of the mirror. She has smeared her mother's lip stick over her mouth. She is soliloquizing, obviously taking the part of her mother talking to her in an incessant stream. She says,

> You see, darling,
> It's the cook's day off
> And I must go to lunch.
> I won't be gone long
> But, my darling, I must go to a party.
> No, don't you scream
> I can't come now
> But I will at five . . .

Why, Shirley!
What's the idea of throwing that coffee out?
My goodness!
For the love of muds . . .
My goodness!
For the love of mikes . . .
Look at this nice coffee I'm making.

Why, Shirley!
Don't get too close
Cause it splatters.
Didn't I tell you
Don't get too close.

Perhaps it seems like a lot of nonsense. "But to me," said Shirley's mother wisely, "it suddenly made a lot of sense."

14. New ways of discipline in our schools

THE WHOLE CHILD GOES TO SCHOOL

Edith sits at her desk staring ahead into space as if she did not want to see or hear what the teacher or anyone else is saying. This is the same Edith whose father repeatedly berates her for her "dumbness" and whose mother is forever criticizing her manners, her looks, her way of talking until now Edith is afraid of opening her mouth. George, with the sullen face and brooding eyes, is always ready to pick a fight and yell "dirty sheeny!" He is the same George whose mother has always threatened to pack him off to boarding school. Her chief method of punishment has been to "isolate" him. Johnny Jones, who stands up in class and recites in meek and mild fashion, an hour before was screaming in a tantrum on the dining-room floor. He is the same Johnny Jones who, an hour later, angrily throws a rock through the school window and goes undiscovered, throwing the blame on another boy.

What good will it do Edith for her teacher to keep on saying, "Speak up, Edith. Sit up and pay attention. Use your eyes. Use your ears. Use your tongue." Because of the emotions inside her, Edith cannot talk. She cannot bear to look squarely at life and the world around her. Hearing and seeing and talking bring too much hurt.

What good will it do for George to sit on a bench in the principal's outer office hour on end while one person after another walks past and away from him, leaving him isolated and alone? This only makes George the more bitterly in

Child: "Sh! That's Miss Cross-patch. The old bag!"
Second child: "What she needs is to join our painting class and get some of her mean feelings out."

need of letting out the resentment inside him. It only piles up the feelings of being deserted which have already brought him so much hurt.

What good will it do to pat Johnny Jones on the back and praise him for his fine recitation, leaving the sly anger to find its own outlet? What good will come to either Johnny Jones or society if he is left without learning to handle the destructive feelings that lurk inside him?

Edith and George and Johnny and millions of other children come to school bringing their emotions with them as well as their bodies and intellects. Edith and George and Johnny have more serious "problems" than many. But the difference lies in degree, not in essence. We know that we can no longer have our schools work only on the mind and ignore the rest of the child. We have gone far since the days when Mario's mother answered his teacher's request to have Mario bathed, with a note saying, "He comes to school for to teach, teacher. He don't come to school for to smell."

In many classrooms today, teachers are helping to meet children's physical needs. They see to it, for example, that those who require it have midmorning milk or midafternoon rest. They recognize that if a child is physically overtired or undernourished, his schoolwork can be readily affected.

In some classrooms today, teachers are helping also to meet children's emotional needs. So far they are few and far between, these teachers. But here and there they are working, alone or in small groups, courageously moving forward, knowing that if a child is emotionally overwrought or undernourished his schoolwork is affected, as is also his personality and his life.

These teachers realize that a child must feel that he is understood and appreciated for what he is as well as for what he accomplishes. They know that it helps a child to study if he feels that he is *wanted* and *belongs* in his classroom. They know that emotional warmth and protection from coldness is just as important as protection from cold winds and draughts. They know that many a disciplinary problem has yielded when the old punitive disciplinary measures have stopped and the new acceptant measures have begun.

Here is eleven-year-old Benton, who has failed in one school and has just been transferred to another. In the school where he had failed, the principal had reported, "He isn't a bad child; that's not the problem. He really is very sweet. He's lackadaisical, though, and lazy. He doesn't want to work and you can't make him. Whatever you say seems to go right over his head. The real trouble is that he isn't as bright as the rest of the children. His I.Q. is only 103, while most in this school run from 115 to 135. So, he really doesn't have much chance!" (As if a child's chance should depend on his ability to compete with other children, rather than on developing whatever he has in himself.)

In the new school, his teacher, Mrs. Waring, watched him with noticing eyes. "He's such a good child," she thought, "it isn't natural." But she had seen too-good children before and knew from her past experience and from her keen awareness that too much goodness might be a cover-up for not-such-good feelings. The school where she taught was in a stable community of upper middle-class homes. The children were "normal" children. There were very few serious behavior problems among them. Some of the children had sleeping difficulties; some bit or picked at their nails or were "fussy eaters" or had tantrums or fought too much with other children. But the chief complaint, as in most places, was the parents' lament that these children were "hard to discipline," "stubborn," "impertinent" and "inconsiderate." The parents, all in all, had done a conscientious job, giving their children every advantage they knew of. But very few had learned as had Mrs. Waring that the held-in, negative, unwelcome and "bad" emotions often choke out the positive ones—the vigorous impulses toward creation and growth.

"Many of these children have so many potentialities and are not developing them simply because they've been taught

218

to hold in so tight! They've learned to handle their minds but not their emotions!"

And so Mrs. Waring had set up her classroom in a way that would help the children bring out their various feelings.

"We have to educate a person's feelings as well as his thinking," she said. "It's no good a man's learning, for example, to make business investments if the knowledge is used to cheat other people. It's no good learning about explosives if the knowledge is put to blowing up the world. We can't let the seeds of strife and dissension, prejudice and war multiply unseen inside our children until they have overgrown the whole of their emotional lives."

Mrs. Waring knew that children must learn to see and to deal with the feelings they have inside—the bad as well as the good. "They must learn to get the bad ones out. For we have discovered in recent years that it's through getting negative feelings out rather than holding them in that we make them diminish. Only, and this is important, certain conditions must be adhered to if the getting out of these negative feelings is to do any good. A child must learn to let out in harmless activities; not in ways that destroy or hurt. He must, furthermore, let out to an understanding, acceptant person who, by the very understanding and acceptance, helps him to feel less driven and desperate, less terrified and rebellious. It's a big order. But since it's these things that enable the more positive feelings to enter and flourish, it's these things that I must give my children the chances to do," she stated.

When Mrs. Waring told the children that they might paint or draw, she did not focus alone on such things as Indian wigwams and Eskimo huts. When she assigned compositions she did not keep to such theses as "How I Spent My Vacation" . . . "The Nicest Day in My Life" . . . or "What I've Discovered about Pioneers." The discoveries were pointed closer to home. "Let's write about how we feel. Or paint or draw about our feelings. About ourselves. The good feelings, the bad feelings; it doesn't matter. Everybody's got both inside him—bad, mean feelings as well as good ones . . . Remembrances of bad things we've done. Bad things we've wanted to do. Mean ways we've felt; perhaps at home, perhaps at school. About different people. Perhaps even about me . . . Hurt ways we've felt. Frightened ways, too. Everybody feels such things."

Benton sat watching while the other children's pencils moved across their sheets. Finally, he, too, wrote. Slowly and painfully.

> I'm not everybody. I think you're bad to put any such ideas in my head.
>
> > Benton.

As was her custom, the teacher read their contributions aloud. "We have a pact," she explained to newcomers. "These things are just between us. Secrets that we share." Eyes sparkled at this point.

One new child said, challengingly, "You don't take bad things to the principal and bench us for them?"

"You're scared that I might. Well, I don't."

"You don't tell our folks?"

"You're worried about that, too. But I don't."

"Okay. Read."

When she read Benton's brief paper, she said, very simply mirroring the feelings he had expressed, "You were mad at me, Benton, for mentioning that people could feel hurt or frightened or mean or bad."

Benton searched her face for condemnation. But he saw only good, warm understanding—the sort of expression that said, "I'm *with* you no matter how you feel!" He knew—inexplicably, but he knew it—that this teacher appreciated how he felt. She wasn't angry even though his antagonism had been directed at her. Perhaps later he could say more. With
220

a sigh of relief he turned to listening to what some of the other children had done.

Edna wrote this one:

> I know a woman who is a slave-driver. She lives right in my home. She makes me slave and toil. It's gone on for years.
>
> This is her fortune. It showed in a cup of tea that a woman told at the pier. Her child would get a shotgun, a blackjack and a huge ubangi club. The results would be wonderful.
> But they never happened because one day she got sick and died. She was buried in the city dump with a monument of bottles and tin cans.

Benton listened while the teacher reflected Edna's feelings. "Edna was very mad at this woman, just like all of us get mad at times with people who make us do things—so mad that we want to kill them dead."

"We can't, of course!" said Edna, practically.

"No, we can't."

"But you know what I've noticed?" said Edna with the deep thoughtfulness of having made a real discovery. "After you write it out, the wanting doesn't make you explode all over the place. The wanting seems to get smaller."

"You feel less like having the madness break out all over after you've written or painted or talked it out here."

"But you get much madder for a while—while you're doing it. You get so mad you think you're going to bust. And then you get over it!" said a fat boy.

"At first you scare yourself like with a ghost," said a tall, thin girl.

"These feelings are like ghosts of things we bury inside us. It's better to unbury them and not be a regular graveyard inside, isn't it?"

A dozen nods.

They're learning to handle their feelings, thought Mrs. Waring. *They're no longer blank and shy about them as they were a couple of months back.* Aloud she continued, "Here's Paula's. She wrote a rhymy sort of verse.

I AM MAD AT MY MOTHER

I can't go to the plunge
Because—
I have to wash my windows
With a sponge.

I'm mad at my mother
She makes me
So blue
Because it's true

I can't go to the plunge
Because—
I have to wash my windows
With that old, smelly sponge.

Paula's mother had reported after the writing of this verse that Paula had curiously turned more cooperative. Edna's mother had reported a decrease in Edna's lies and a growing kind of consideration. *It does work,* thought Mrs. Waring once more, wondering what it would do for Benton.

As the days rolled around and Benton saw how other children brought out their feelings, he grew less hesitant in bringing out his. First came a story about the fears that he had been shutting in.

I shouldn't be afraid to be alone in the house at night but I sure am. I turn on the radio but somehow the floor creaks louder than the music and I feel like a regular screwball for getting goose pimples but—gosh—I do. I swallow it down and try to keep it in but it only comes out in goose pimples. I get so d—— mad at myself I could cry.

"You got so mad at yourself for being afraid," Mrs. Waring accepted what Benton had said.

The next thing he turned in said something different. It was a painting done in black poster paints. All heavy and black. Two great giantlike people were in it: a man and a woman and down in one corner a small, bent figure, apparently a child. And spread all over the sheet, slanting and straight, in big and small letters, very black, was the one command: DON'T. Two dozen "don'ts" at least on the paper.

"Want to tell us about it?" asked Mrs. Waring.

Benton shook his head.

"Rather write about it?"

Benton's face brightened. He wrote swiftly and brought the paper and put it into Mrs. Waring's hand.

DON'T

> There are two million don'ts actually in my house. Many of them are justifiable. But an awful lot aren't. Don't they remember at all about when they were children? You don't want to walk a tight-rope all the time like in a circus, afraid to put your foot in the wrong place. I don't want to be a tight-rope walker. I want to be a lion and roar and growl and fight. I'm MAD.

When Mrs. Waring read this she again mirrored Benton's feelings by saying, "Benton's mad at all the don'ts."

"Who isn't?" said another boy.

"That's when I want to kill them," said still another.

Mrs. Waring, glancing at Benton, barely caught his next words, they were murmured so low. "I could kill them too."

During the year much of the same thing went on. Benton's anger came out stronger and stronger until there was room enough for other, more positive feelings to enter. More drive and push toward accomplishment. More contact with other people. More laughter. More zest. Benton's work was the work of a person who wanted to work, who wanted to grapple with problems outside him since the problems inside were no longer so intense. There was no such thing as failure now in Benton's life. His intelligence was no longer bound by held-in anger and fear. It was free to function as was shown, for one thing, by his I.Q. It had risen from 103 to 142. "Just another indication," said Mrs. Waring, "that held-in negative feelings can spoil whatever a person does—even his thinking—and that getting negative feelings out under proper conditions *can* and does help."

LEADING THE WAY

Benton is just one of the many children who have improved with such treatment. Here is Lester, eight, who was a "reading problem" until he had gotten out his feelings of anger against his mother and the grandparents who lived near him. "They sit and sit and look like funerals" . . . "They make my mother get all hunched up with hurry to go out whenever they come around" . . . "I hate them. I don't blame her for running away" . . . "I hate my mother, too. When she runs away she leaves them to put the big stick on me."

Here is Eva, in high school, doing poorly. "Not college material" in a family where the college tradition was strong. But Eva turned out to be college material after she had worked with a wonderful teacher in the arts and crafts room. To Mrs. Knight, Eva was not just one of the two hundred pupils. Eva was Eva. Said Mrs. Knight, "I don't know what sort of background Eva has. I wish I did but it doesn't seem possible in our school. However, I do know how Eva feels when she's with me and I'm able to feel with her and accept her feelings and help her to get more of them out in her paintings and in the work she does with clay. Among Eva's pictures were a whole series done in chalk in primitive blocks of color. Always three figures hanging on gibbets. In the first picture they were far in the distance. They came closer. In the last picture they were in the foreground: "a proud father, a tempestuous mother and the vilest brother you ever saw. What's wrong with him? He's perfect. There's never anything wrong. That's what's wrong. I'd like to wring his neck."

Connie's picture of her brother is a bit less violent. Connie

224

is six and in a first grade with thirty-four other children. Her brother is two. Connie's long-suffering mother had complained to Miss Millford saying, "She never concentrates, teacher. I don't know how you're going to handle her." When the discussion turned, as do all discussions sooner or later, to "troubles I'm having at home," Connie talked at length about her small brother. Finally, she painted his portrait. A toddler with one end of a heavy rope around his middle, the other end tied firmly to the trunk of a tree. "That'll fix him," said Connie. Laboriously, then, she added a title in big red letters across the bottom of the sheet: THE NOOSANS. "That's what he is," she said.

As ordinarily happens, when Connie had let out enough of the feelings that had put her mind into a jumble, her mind was a jumble no more. "How did you do it, Miss Millford? She's gotten so she can *think!*"

The Mrs. Warings and Mrs. Knights and Miss Millfords are rare. But, fortunately, they exist and, fortunately, through patient exploration they have found ways of overcoming the difficulties of helping children to develop emotionally as well as intellectually in spite of crowded quarters and too large a teaching load. They are realizing that this is not only the best way of handling incipient problems but also a reducer of disciplinary ills.

In a kindergarten with sixty-nine children, the two unusual teachers somehow find time enough for the affection that all small children need and without which the release of feelings would serve less purpose. "We can even manage 'time alone' snatched in little quickies," said one of the teachers. "An arm about a child, a smile and a listening ear in answer to his telling about a picture. Then a private kind of reflection of his feelings alone. It's done in a few moments and for the shy ones seems to serve even better than what's said in the group."

In a class of twenty-five "retarded" children ten and eleven years old, an outstanding teacher has time to know and understand and feel with each child. From her own report, she knows that "Robert's father, having deserted the family for years, has just returned; the mother was an inmate in a state hospital for a while and is harsh to the point of cruelty. Robert is surly, aggressive, can sign slips sent to his mother. Does practically no work. Anna Lee is youngest of fourteen children, most of them married with families of their own. The mother is an old woman, the father old too. Anna Lee worries, does not mix or play with other children, loves to help the teacher, is sullen, fights a great deal. The father beats her until welts appear. . . ." A group of serious problems exist in this room. Difficult children. And yet, more eager and gentler as they get their feelings out and as their remarkably fine teacher accepts and understands.

Among the procedures were discussions of things that were happening at home and of the mean feelings that resulted, the acting out of some of the happenings in simple scenes which the children made up spontaneously as they went along. Then, too, the children drew and cut out paper-doll puppets of the chief tormentors in life. "The cruel grandmothers, the bullying father, big brothers taking candy from babies, mothers, sisters, neighbors, storekeepers. And we made these puppets act out family dramas. . . .

"We also drew funnies; a series of what we didn't like, what people did to us, what happened to us . . . And we had bean bags with which to pelt blackboard pictures of people who 'make us feel mad or mean.' "

Among the pictures painted were "pretty mothers with long sticks," "fathers with clubs," "fires burning them up" and "mud and rocks hitting them."

But there was no license in this classroom. Action, in many instances, had to be redirected or curtailed even though anything went as far as the *admission of feelings* was concerned. If children fought with each other, for instance, the fighting
226

was stopped, but they drew pictures of the offender on the blackboard and pelted it with the bean bags.

In a junior high school group of all Negro children, many of the hurt and resentful feelings came out with the help of another gifted teacher.

Wrote Lilly:

> I dislike eviction notices. During the war we got one and we had to move right then. None of us have been right since. We can't live right.
>
> . . . . .
>
> I don't like evictions.

Wrote Frank:

> Demerits—
> They are awful,
> Also the quiet teacher
> Who, without warning,
> Gives you an "F" for the day's work
> If you borrow a pencil
> Or chew gum.
> And the teacher who piles homework
> On you, and, if you complain
> You're reminded,
> "There's room for one more
> In Special Guidance."
> Then there's the one
> Who always reminds you
> Of your heritage and background.
> And if you answer back
> You get
> *Detention.*

Still another rare teacher has a kindergarten with twenty children in a substantial middle-class stable community. Chances for release run all through the day. When opportunity was first presented to paint out mean feelings, fifteen of the twenty went to it. One unhappy child made a daddy of clay and beat him up with a stick until nothing but a mass

227

remained. Another drowned everyone he knew in the ocean he painted. "I'll show you how mean I feel. I want to throw everybody in the water."

This teacher, too, had limitations on what the children might *do*. Actions that went too far or were too loud and wild, actions that disturbed the peace of the building or were destructive or hurtful in any way had to be stopped.

Billy, for instance, was all for using his BB gun. "You're feeling real mean," his feelings were accepted and reflected. "You want to shoot people. But that won't do." His actions were curtailed. There were no long explanations; no reasoning why on and on. There was simply the simple statement of law. "But you *can* get your mean feelings out by drawing whom you'd like to shoot or in any other picture you'd like. . . ." The feelings were rechanneled into a form where they would find a normal outlet instead of doing injury or harm.

In other words, this teacher—as all of us must—had rules that needed to be adhered to. There could not be too much noise. Paper for finger paints could be spread only on the linoleum rug. Hammer and saw had to stay at the workbench. There could be no running in the halls. These and other rules had to be heeded. But this teacher found, as did the others, that penalties and punishments, rewards and merits were not needed to enforce the rules. The mere reiteration of them from time to time as they were forgotten was enough to keep the children in line.

The fact that the children's feelings had been understood made the difference. The teacher's acceptance brought increased cooperation in its wake.

Playhouse corners in nursery school, kindergarten and first grade have provided many opportunities for feelings to come out and be released. Says Mamie, five, "Ena's the mama and I'm the baby. I get hurt and now I'm resting. Mama fusses over me and I beam."

228

Still another wonderful teacher recounts her experience after reading a story of "Snow White" to her class. "I stopped just past the part where the wicked witch comes into the story. 'Say, we'd all like to do bad things, just the way the witch did, wouldn't we?'

"A shout of gleeful agreement.

" 'Well,' I went on cautiously, 'do you suppose . . . we could all tell each other about some of those mean things we've done or have seen others do? . . . Because so many of us have done these things it makes us feel better to tell about them. . . .'

"The circle of children around me tightened in. Some could scarcely keep from falling off their chairs as each hurried the other up, poking and thumping the current teller in the anxiety to tell his own story. My pencil moved across my paper in a rhythm as excited as the children's voices as they talked out their stories . . . Hurt feelings about their families came out quickly, poisonously acute. . . .

> One child pathetically told how her father had lured her on with "Come here, I'll give you a piece of candy," and then had used the razor strap on her instead.
>
> Another told how, when her little sister got a new mattress and no one else in the family had one, she had poured a bottle of mercurocrome all over it.

"During our art period, working with clay, I stood back again and listened and wrote. 'What shall we make, Miss?' the children asked, afraid at first.

" 'Why, anything you wish. You want to get used to the feeling of clay today . . . how good and squishy it is between your fingers . . . how you can poke and thump it and do anything with it. You may not wish to make anything at all.'

"Of course some of them did, proudly rolling out 'tortillas' or 'baskets' or 'a little dog to take home and show my mother.' But from the largest part of the group I heard pent-up feelings coming out . . . such as one boy shouting, 'Shut up or I'll clunk you with a stick' as he smashed a clay strip against the table. Others were shooting each other down with clay airplanes or zooming into each other with clay submarines. Many just delighted in the feel of the clay all period, sliding, swishing, and dabbling in it. And then there was Virginia, who had worked in silence and who held up a knobby ball with clay globs projecting from it, with 'Look . . . a man murdering a girl.' I just nodded and smiled at her in confidence that it was all right."

In spite of the horror, the teacher knew that it was far better for Virginia to get her feelings out onto a soft lump of clay than to hold them in a tight hard lump in her heart. Virginia had been attacked not so far back, and the memory was like the memory of murder. Letting it come out now in this way had value. This showed in the look of immeasurable relief that followed—"the first look of peace I'd ever seen on Virginia's face!" With more of the same sort of outlet Virginia began to shed her moroseness and ugly defiance. "But I had not preached or scolded. I had tried simply to understand!"

As usually happens, the children here showed more and more of their positive side as the negative feelings were released and accepted. A boy who had been caught time and again carrying a knife in his shirt and whose frown had been as deep as a scar between his eyes, began carrying roses to school. "For you, Miss." The first positive gesture toward contact he'd ever been known to make. A girl who had sullenly sat during every cleanup time with a "stomach-ache so bad I can't move," began pitching in with vigor. A perpetual fighter had miraculously given up fighting and had for the first time in his life begun to laugh and chat with other children. A prejudiced youngster who had used every available opportunity to hurl the word "nigger" at the colored children invited one of the Negro boys to come onto his team. All positive actions—these.

The punitive program that had been operating in the lives of these youngsters for years had failed to effect such changes. The children had been getting worse, not better. Then the new type of program with the new type of discipline had been started. "For a while they were worse, as they usually are. They went overboard in expressing all kinds of 'murder'— like Virginia's man murdering the girl. Only with most of them it grew out of the anger they had held inside." The limitations which the teacher put on certain actions had to be repeatedly stated. "But, strangely, even the children who had been most recalcitrant began soon to heed what was said. For, at one and the same time—and for the first time in their lives —their feelings were being permitted, accepted and understood. Gradually, bit by bit, then, more wholesome and positive things came to life." So avows this teacher.

With her and with the other teachers, the whole child goes to school. Not just his intellect. Not just his body. His emotions go too. As the troubled emotions are released and accepted, they grow less intense and another part of emotional living has a chance to come into being and flourish. The part of him that sends him sizzling like a sky rocket in bursts of enthusiasm, the part that propels him to tackle hard tasks and to stick them out, the part that stirs him to paint lovely pictures, the part that moves him to tenderness and warmth.

Part Four

Moving ahead

15. Mechanical measures or creative endeavors?

NOT ENOUGH RECIPES

One person steps into a kitchen and day after day, year after year, pulls out the same recipes and meticulously follows each detail. Another steps in and mixes a little of this, a little of that, feeling his way as he goes. On first appearance it looks as if the latter were cooking "by instinct." Actually, his dishes turn out well because he has become familiar and comfortable with the basic rules and finds it challenging and interesting from there on to experiment with the materials that come to his hand.

As parents we dare not remain recipe-followers. There just are not enough recipes to go around the clock to fit every moment, every situation, every parent, every child, every mood, every child-parent-mood-hour combination.

One grownup uses certain words with a certain child and the results are like magic. Another grownup uses the same words with the same child and the results are nil. The child's reaction to these two big people is different. Or the same grownup uses the selfsame words with two different children and again there are different results. What happens in each instance is the sum of many subtle things. Tiredness enters. Mood. And the general rapport or relationship that exists. It's the same when two adults are together. Says one woman to another, "If my husband talked to me the way your husband talks to you, I'd walk out the front door." "But your husband isn't my husband," says the other, smiling to herself with a Mona Lisa expression as if this explained all.

Take a child. Take a parent or teacher. Take a "naughty

Mother [perturbed]: "Haven't I told you a million times not to lose your temper?"
Son: "That's just the trouble. The other guy lost it. Mine's still inside."

act." Take a recipe for cure. Mix them all together and you'll get NO EXACT RESULT.

There is no one simple recipe
by which we can go.

A worried mother sent a letter. "Please write a book," she pleaded, "that will list *every problem* and give a step-by-step method for handling it correctly. You could arrange it alphabetically. Then when my child spits I can quickly turn to

'Spitting'; when he hits, to 'Hitting'; when he wets, to 'Wetting'; and when he gets saucy, to 'Sauces.' I think that would *really* help." We can picture her Johnny screaming on the floor while she runs for the book and flips the pages to the mechanical, step-by-step method she seeks.

At one time, spanking was supposed to be the answer to all problems. You spanked for every crime on every occasion. That was DISCIPLINE. Simple. Easy. When a child was "bad" you acted automatically. There was no need to *think*. But today we are not satisfied with spanking. We know also that there is no one thing to take spanking's place. There are, however, BASIC PRINCIPLES. When we are familiar with these and get the feel and the hang of them, then we can use them here, use them there, adapt them, change them, shape them to fit. We can use them CREATIVELY instead of mechanically. There is challenge to this.

The new discipline takes us away from the insensitivity of automatic, mechanical measures. It calls on the finest and deepest and most human qualities in us. It calls for sympathy, for feeling *with* another person, for *accepting* in contrast to *condemning*, for faith in a child's push toward wholeness. It reaches down for the creative spark that each and every one of us has.

When we stop to think, "Which will it be—the mechanical or the creative way?" we have only one answer. The latter, of course.

But still we may find ourselves pulling back and turning aside. "It's too indefinite!" . . . "It permits too much license!" . . . "It doesn't train a child to obey!" These and countless further objections may keep on rising. And yet, in the back of our minds we still find ourselves searching. We want *something* to answer our questions on discipline. The old ways don't work. But we are not quite convinced that we should accept these new ones.

Let us ask ourselves why.

BLIND SPOTS

We all know about blind spots. When we drive a car we don't expect to possess the perfect vision that sweeps the entire landscape, revealing all. But when we turn to the far more difficult job of rearing a child, we discover that we have expected just this of ourselves. We've expected too much.

We are bound to have had blind spots through all the days and years of his growing. There have been things we have not seen, things we have not done, things we have not known, things we have not been able to feel. Perhaps by looking into ourselves now with as great honesty as we can muster, we will be able to penetrate some of the shadows and see where we have not seen before.

This will take sincerity. It will take courage. At least some of the answers which we bring out of our self-searching may hurt our pride. They may deflate us. They may make us sad for the time being. But not for long.

Always, as a person sees clearly, the task ahead grows less threatening. Hesitance and doubt are lessened. New strength is born.

PROBING THE SHADOWS

Fear is the greatest offender. It causes most of our emotional blind spots. We are afraid, and often without knowing it, of facing many things. And yet, when we have once looked squarely at them, we find that their danger diminishes much as the fear of an imagined burglar vanishes from the wavering shadow in a dark corner of a room as soon as we turn on the light.

And so we will do well to ask ourselves, "What are we afraid of in these new ways of disciplining? Do these new ways carry threats for us that we have not even suspected might be there?"

238

Am I afraid if I admit that my child has hurt or fearful or angry feelings I am owning up to his being a "problem child?"

Have I had the mistaken idea that if a child is "normal," he won't have fearful or hurt feelings? And, most important, have I believed falsely that if he has "mean" feelings, something is wrong?

The truth is that all children in our culture do have "mean" feelings. They also have hurts and fears. They would be abnormal, insensitive little brutes if they didn't, since such feelings are the natural and most healthy reactions to the kinds of things that they have encountered in life, especially during their first two years. There is no cause for us to worry about such feelings unless they are present in overabundance. We know that these emotions are to be expected, for we've been talking about *normal* children all through this book. One of our major concerns in bringing up a child is to keep an overabundance of such feelings from developing. Another major concern is to help him handle these normal feelings in a normal manner so that abnormal problems do not result.

We know now that getting feelings out—releasing them through harmless channels and having them accepted—is the safest and soundest way.

During the last war our soldiers were taught that fear was normal. To admit and own up to their fear enabled them to be more courageous. We do well to apply the same principle to our children. Getting the negative feelings out helps the positive feelings to grow. That a child needs release of "mean" feelings does not signify that he's a problem.

ALL CHILDREN NEED RELEASE AND ACCEPTANCE OF "MEAN" FEELINGS.

ALL CHILDREN HAVE "MEAN" FEELINGS THAT NEED TO BE RELEASED.

As we admit and permit and help a child steer the negative feelings, *problems are prevented*. He has more chance of staying normal as he grows.

Am I afraid that I'll be looked on as a problem parent?

> Do I feel that any "naughtiness" my child shows, any lack of manners, any messiness, noisiness or disobedience marks him as a problem child?

> Then—having heard the adage that a problem child always spells a problem parent—am I perhaps afraid that latter term applies to me?

> Then, do I quickly hustle to make my child into a better obeyer, forgetting his needs, his hurts, his fears in order to prove that I myself am not a problem?

Perhaps we need to ask instead, "How about a problem public? Isn't it time people stop labeling a child as a problem for the perfectly natural, normal childness he shows?"

Am I perhaps still afraid of my neighbors' criticism?

> Am I afraid perhaps of the people who live next door? Of the people who come to visit? Of the teacher who teaches in the next classroom and keeps her children mousy-quiet and who never has any messy moments to mar the meticulous neatness?

> Am I afraid they will raise their hands and their eyebrows and think less well of me because they see me letting my child mess? Because they see me tolerant of his tears? Because they see me responding to his querulous whining with an answer to his feelings rather than with sharpness of tongue?

Am I afraid these people will say, "What a spoiled brat!" . . . *"What terrible parents!"* . . . *"Just look at him; his parents have absolutely no control."*

Am I perhaps afraid of offending or displeasing my own parents?

Am I worried that they will think I'm not doing a good job with my child?

Do I find myself wanting my child to be "extra" good when they come around? Wanting to show how smart he is? What he can do well? And wanting him, conversely, not to do any of the "naughty things" we know are naughty but natural?

We must remember that, without realizing it, we often do hold little-child parts in ourselves. One of these little-child parts lies in needing to have continuous approval from our own parents even though we're grown up. It's hard then to say in adult fashion if we must, "Our ideas are not the same as yours. We've learned different ways of bringing up children. But this does not mean that we're disloyal to you. We can and do still love you even though we differ. After all, differences of opinion and differences in ways of doing things do not need to stand for falling out with one another."

If we ourselves feel all right inside about departing from our parents' precepts, we may find that mirroring their objections is as effective a phase of the new discipline as mirroring what our children feel.

Am I afraid of my own self-criticism?

Does this have a familiar sort of ring? Have other things in the past affected me the same way? Have I had a kind

241

of haunting fear of not doing things well enough? Of not being quite adequate?

Remember those old "inferiority feelings"? Have they bothered me in the past? Do they bother me still?

Without our knowing it, those inferiority feelings may be working overtime in regard to bringing up our children. Without our knowing it, every time a child does something naughty we may feel that we ourselves are failing. And, quickly, we may try to cover our inferiority by proving to ourselves that we are big and powerful in that we *can* make a child mind.

We may find ourselves worrying that if he gripes or grumbles or protests or expresses anger or resentment, he will be called "spoiled." That throws us back into our old sense of inferiority. It spoils our sense of achievement. We begin to feel we haven't brought him up as we should.

We need to remember that the more he holds in his resentments and protests, the more uncooperative he'll feel. He may mind, but his minding can well be because he fears what we may do to him.

This poses quite a problem. We've come to believe that he will feel more positive after he's gotten out his resentment. We know that he will then act more as we ask because he wants to. But while he's getting out his resentment we'll have to cope with our own fear of condemnation, since many people will fail to tolerate our tolerance of him. That old sense of "inferiority" will be hit. In the face of this dilemma we do well to ask, "Sacrificing our own prowess or his progress —which shall it be?"

Am I afraid that my child's resentment may mean he doesn't love me?

Am I afraid if he is even the least bit angry at me, calls me names, says he hates me, that this proves he doesn't care for me at all?

242

Have I forgotten that in our culture when a child is small he ordinarily has to suffer many frustrations?

Am I losing sight of the fact that I had to impose those frustrations on my child, since mine was the task of training him during his earliest years?

Have I forgotten that hostility is not only a natural result but also the very healthiest type of response to frustration?

Isn't it true that I had no information on how to handle his resentments when he was small? Wasn't it natural for me to prod and punish for what I thought was naughtiness and nothing more?

So now I can see—can't I?—that his hostility piled up also as a *natural* result.

But, most important, have I failed to understand that love and hate *can* and *do* go together? That *resentment does not deny loving?*

That just because a child expresses hostility, it does not mean that he cannot also love the person to whom he is hostile?

Isn't it true that we ourselves are apt to be more resentful to someone whom we love than to someone for whom we don't care a mite? A man says in typical fashion, "Why does my wife make me so mad? If I didn't care so much about her, I wouldn't mind. It's because I do care that she gets under my skin."

We can hate heartily one moment and love deeply the next. We can be angry and at the same time deeply in love.

243

We can feel the surge of resentment rise and know simultaneously that a strong steady current of warm affection flows underneath.

No matter what we have done, no matter how hard we may try now, we cannot obviate all hostility in a child as he grows. The best we can do is to help him learn to meet and handle it. All through his life he will have moments of being hurt, of being fearful, of being angry.

Helping him learn how to handle these feelings—how to face them, release them, rechannel them—this is one of the biggest and most important things we can do for him. For his own sake and for the sake of all those with whom his life intertwines. As we do this, we will find that he *loves us much better* even though his moments of "hating" are openly declared.

We can know, too, that when a child is able to show his resentment directly to us, he is simultaneously evidencing confidence in us. The more he can *be as he really is* and *show us how he really feels,* the more truly does he trust us. He doesn't have to use subterfuge and hide himself from us. He knows that we will accept him, feel with him and understand.

Must I still condemn a child's anger and resentment for fear that hostility—especially to a parent—is wicked and wrong?

Are we perhaps still driven by the childhood teachings we ourselves had? Are we still afraid that loving and honoring parents cannot enter where hostility exists, forgetting, as we have just said, that they can go together?

Are we still remembering our own childhood guilt when the least hostility to our own parents crept in?

Can we recall saying to ourselves in the solitary misery of not being understood, "I'll show them. I'll run away so they'll be sorry!" (This was our own resentment!) Can we remember then how quickly repentance followed? How we grew sorry that such wicked thoughts should be in us? And how we rushed to do nice things in order to be forgiven?

Many times there was such anxiety in us as children when we were hostile that now all unwittingly we try to cover up the fact that we were ever hostile. Altogether unconsciously, then, we may steer away from our child's aggression as from a red-hot poker. It reminds us too much of our own unremembered aggression. It's as if we said to ourselves, "If I admit that *my* child feels that way, I'm admitting that *any* child can feel that way and that's admitting that I, too, might have felt that way as a child. The mere thought is too horrible! I've got to pull the shade down and not even look at the possibility. I can't let my child express any animosity. I've got to punish it out of him fast.

"If I admit it's natural in him, I also admit it was natural in me. It may, in fact, still be inside me—a remnant of the child-part that lies in us all. . . ." The crux of the matter is that *it's hard to look at feelings in a child that we've always looked away from in ourselves.*

And so, whenever he shows animosity, we are apt to rush in with suggestions that he cover up and hide his mean feelings. We keep telling him to be loving and sweet. "You mustn't say bad things to mommie. She's a nice mommie. She loves you and does things for you."

We keep telling ourselves that we must encourage constructive feelings, forgetting that positive, warm feelings come, not when hostility is denied, but when it is faced and worked off. We forget the all-important truth that to be rid of poison, it must come out and not remain festering within.

245

Am I still afraid if I permit my child to bring out his "mean" feelings he'll get into the habit of being mean?

Am I afraid that if I let him express such feelings it will fix them and make them more permanent?

We are apt to keep asking, "Shan't I teach him that such feelings are wrong? Shan't I *encourage* him to express 'nice' feelings instead of the 'mean' ones? Won't the nice feelings automatically replace the mean ones if he does this?" We've had an idea that if a child wants to pinch his baby brother the thing to do is to say, "See, the baby's so sweet! So helpless! It's nice to be nice to him!" . . . By putting a whole array of positive thoughts to the fore, we've believed that he'll forget the negative ones. What really happens is that he covers up and goes right on feeling the mean feelings. He gets the habit of hiding, of SUBTERFUGE, of DECEIT, of HYPOCRISY.

On the other hand, if we help him face and liquidate his feelings, he gets the habit of HONESTY and TRUTHFULNESS. He gets the habit not only of seeing but *handling his mean feelings without doing actual hurt or harm.*

Am I, perhaps, afraid of change?

Do I feel that change is somehow threatening? That it will leave me helpless? That I won't be able to handle things unless I keep on with the old ways even though they have failed to work?

Changing is hard! It's hard to go forward onto a road we've always heard was dark and dangerous, even though someone assures us now that it's the safest path.

There's an insecure feeling about it that frightens us so that we cling shakily to the familiar ways no matter how bumpy they have proved. Unconsciously, we even invent reasons why it would be useless to change. "He's just like

246

his father!" . . . "He's like my mother" . . . "Like my great uncle's aunt!" As if this explained everything and gave us reason to think that no matter how much we changed, he'd still be hopeless! "You can't change inheritance! You can't make a silk purse out of a sow's ear!"

Or we may find ourselves offering another type of excuse: "I have too much to do and the new discipline is too time consuming. I can't manage, for instance, to have twenty minutes or half an hour of 'time alone' with each of my three children. Even twice a week is too much. I just can't make it. There just *isn't* the time."

If we find ourselves offering this kind of protest, we'll do well to try a little experiment. Keep record of the time we spend now running after a child, scolding him, yelling at him, trying to enforce obedience, bribing him, reasoning with him, fighting with him to mind. Doesn't it come to more than twenty or thirty minutes a day? The new way in discipline is time consuming. So is the old way. Only we forget.

Am I afraid it's too late to start with new methods?

Do I fear that I've done such irreparable harm by using the wrong methods that adopting new ways now would serve no purpose?

Actually, *it's never too late.* A child may have built up many hurts and fears and hostility. But this does not mean it's too late to change. It simply means we'll have more to help him work through. It means that we'll need to try more diligently, that we'll need to be as clear as we can in ourselves, that we'll need to have deep courage to meet things. We may need and want to seek outside, professional help to feel stronger and more secure.*

* If you are in need of this kind of help and do not know where to find it, write to the National Committee for Mental Hygiene, 1790 Broadway, New York 19, N.Y., and ask where you might inquire nearer home. Don't forget either, that the physical and psychological interact. Be sure to have a physical check by your doctor or pediatrician.

Am I afraid to admit that I haven't perhaps given my child what I should have given him?

If I admit his hurt feelings, his fears and his resentments, won't this bring proof that I haven't met all his needs?

Do I keep arguing, "It's nonsense to think that we haven't given him everything! We have. He's had EVERY ADVANTAGE. There's not a thing that he's lacked."

If we find ourselves protesting that we *have* met all our child's needs, we may unwittingly be trying to cover up a fear that we have not given him quite as much as we tell ourselves. This covering-up act is very common. Many of us do it. It hurts us too much to admit that we have not fully met his needs.

Actually, no parents can completely meet their children's needs. (This we have seen before and we do well to reiterate.) Lack of knowledge may stand in the way, lack of understanding, and, more important, the blind spots that all of us have. We may carry unconscious child parts in us which we do not see but which still make us unable to give our children the emotional support, the security and the acceptance they need. Even so, the situation is not irreparable! In today's world we have come to know that seeking professional help is not the "disgrace" it was thought to be earlier. We are seeing more and more clearly that, instead of labeling us "crazy," it marks us as all the wiser and more sane.

Am I afraid I won't have anything left to help me make him mind if I give up the idea of rewards and punishments? Of persuasion and reasoning?

Have I been relying on props?
What sort of props? Aren't they pretty weak ones? As if

248

gold-paper stars were something sturdier and more to be counted on than love and understanding! As if a big stick or a stick of candy held greater strength than the strength that comes from a child's deep knowledge that we are *with* him, that we appreciate his feelings—the darkness in him as well as the sunshine and light.

Do I still fear that if I permit and accept his troublesome feelings I automatically permit and accept the troublesome acts?

It *is* hard to differentiate between *action* and *feeling*. But we can if we try. And we find that such differentiation grows easier as we go along. We find, too, that it brings its own rewards. The child's attitude toward us changes. Because we understand him, he wants to understand us. He is more eager to mind. Says Ellen, eight, "It's been so much easier to mind since you've been a mother and not a slugger. Why didn't you start it long ago?"

But in the beginning it will be rough going. It's easier reading than doing!" one woman said. It is. So—let's not be discouraged if we can't put it all into practice all at once. We can't with piano playing, either, or with golf or tennis.

One thing that can help: When you're puzzled, read this book over. It will mean far more after you've tried what's in it than it did before. More than once you will comment: "This answers just what I was wondering about and didn't notice the first time. I never knew it was there!"

This is true:

> The more we accept a child's
> FEELINGS, the more will he accept
> our RULES.

16. Our feelings count too

In some strange fashion during the past years we've gotten a picture of the *good parent* or the *good teacher* as a perfectly poised, ever-calm, serene-faced person who never gets excited, never gets "ruffled," is always placid and sweet.

Miss Blank who teaches in first grade is an excellent example. She smiles serenely on the rows of heads bent over desks. "Half of the children are working on their reading workbooks; half of them are having a free drawing period," she explains in her low, well-modulated voice to the visitor. "They're such a dear little bunch. No problems at all!"

"Yes, Ernestine!" she says, acknowledging the raised hand. Ernestine comes up on mincing feet. "See my picture, Miss Blank. It's a sunset!"

"That's lovely, Ernestine! Yes, Nicholas."

Nicholas comes up in quiet decorum. "I've got this page done now, Miss Blank."

"That's lovely, Nicholas. Lisa Beth, sit up straighter, my dear," she says, the smile no whit dimmer. "It's not good to get your eyes so near the paper. Yes, John."

John comes up and sticks out his paper in shy embarrassment.

"That's lovely, John."

Ernestine's hand once more. "Yes, Ernestine," Miss Blank keeps on smiling graciously.

"Sonny's pulling my hair."

"You can be a nice boy, Sonny." The smile still shining.

Tony's hand; Tony's paper: "A house with a road leading up to it."

"That's lovely, Tony."

Celia's hand. "A mother dog and a baby dog."

"That's lovely, Celia."

Victor's hand and his shuffle up to the front of the room. "See my picture of all hell breaking loose."

"It's love. . . ." The voice stops short for an instant but the smile beams on. "I think you can draw a prettier picture."

The visitor looks up. It's true, Miss Blank's benignness is nothing daunted. In her voice there is still the unruffled calm.

The bell rings for recess.

On the playground the visitor overhears Ernestine saying, smirking, "Isn't Miss Blank just darling?"

Then Lisa Beth with a puzzled frown and keen intuitive perception says a wonderful thing. "She just isn't real, is she?"

The visitor nods to herself: if Miss Blank were real with that smile and that sweetness and the way nothing bothers her, she'd be a *monster*.

Imagine going through life, unfeeling, without emotion. One could commit murder and not feel it. One could be knocked over by a car and not care. "Oh yes, my leg was crippled but it doesn't matter; I'm just as happy." . . . "Oh yes, I murdered him, but since he's better off that way, it doesn't bother me a bit."

The person who lives most fully for others as well as for himself—*feels*. And he lets those who are close feel his feelings with him.

"Nothing drives me so wild," says one young wife, gritting her teeth, "as when my husband sits there. Never opening his mouth or growing the least bit excited no matter how much I rant and rave."

"When I get angry, my husband just blinks and goes to sleep. It makes me twice as mad. I'd like to take a lamp and wake him up in a hurry. And I don't mean by lighting the light in his face."

"When mine shuts his jaws tight and says, 'That's all there is to that; I refuse to argue!' then I feel stricken and helpless. There's nothing to grapple with. It makes things much worse."

The sense of having nothing with which to grapple! We all know it. We've experienced the defeating quality of the icy, smooth calm that one cannot get through. It's like beating against a stone image instead of thrashing things out with another human being in full-blooded, hearty fashion, attempting to find a common meeting ground.

"I'd much rather he'd beat me up than have him turn over and snore."

BE YOURSELF

Actually, there is no such thing as a normal person who doesn't *feel*. Part of being normal is to have feelings that are appropriate to the moment. Part of being normal is to have feelings that come out appropriately.

When a person seems to be emotionless, what he is doing is holding in. Lila, who is seven, detects the storm behind her mother's emotional calm.

> You feel all angry on the inside
> But nothing's coming out of you.
> You *seem* quiet
> But you're not.

Says Roland, nine, whose mother has learned by hard effort to maintain a calm surface, "Oh, you! Your old innocent face makes me so mad. I wish you'd break it up."

Children sense the real feelings behind the superficial expression. Molly's mother smiles sweetly and says in a gentle voice to her four-year-old, "Don't touch the flowers, please, Molly."

Molly looks up with sullen anger. "I won't. But you don't need to lie about wanting to pinch me."

"I've never pinched her in my life," said her mother later.

252

"I've wanted to though. Only I've stopped and hidden it. I guess the hiding is the same as a lie."

When we hide our feelings from our children they sense an insincerity in us which may make them feel we are lying. In essence we are. Although we are not *telling* them an untruth, we are *acting out* an untruth to them. We are employ-

Junior: "Now, Mommie, don't *you* be naughty. Wipe that look off your face."

ing subterfuges and pretenses. We are being more or less hypocritical, actually. We are not only giving our children an example in such modes of behavior. We are being dishonest with them. This they sense.

They may feel then that they can't quite trust us—just as we feel that we can't quite trust people who employ subterfuges and counterfeits, who are hypocritical and not quite honest with us and in whom we sense an attempt to hide things and to keep us out.

"I'd rather have my dad sizzling mad than cold sober!" said eight-year-old Eric sagely. When asked what he meant by "cold sober," he elaborated. "Like when he gets frozen-faced-mad. He never says anything mean or bad. He never gets loud. Just cold. And he pretends like he's pleasant. I wish he'd be like Bob's father, full of yells and cusses. It'd be a relief."

Strange as it may seem, children are more comfortable with yells and cusses than they are with a mask of serenity super-imposed over a grim scowl. They can comprehend the ob-vious anger in a temper tantrum or the open hostility in one person's yelling at another. These are simple expressions on their own level.

Maria, a graceful and charming young woman, describes a typical scene from her childhood with obvious delight. "They were warm and gay at moments. At other moments there were roars of thunder all through the house. I don't know which I remember with most relish. One day I came home from school across the fields. From down the road I heard it. Mama and papa were at it again. When I opened the door, there they were—papa shouting, mama shrieking; papa banging his fists on the table, mama gesticulating wildly; the children lined up on either side, some on mama's team, some on papa's, laughing and cheering.

" 'Mama scored that one! Go to it, Mama.'

" 'Papa, you give her what she deserves!'

"Finally the four-year-old handed mama the thirteen-year-old's baseball bat. 'Here, Mama. Use this.'

"Mama turned on him, bursting into laughter. 'That would never do, angel! You are a very bad boy to tempt me with this!' And she picked him up and gave him a bear hug.

" 'So, Mama, you got chicken feet,' shouted papa, bursting into loud guffaws. Then he came around the table and hugged her.

" 'You mean she's chicken-hearted,' the studious one corrected.

" 'All is one thing,' papa beamed. 'Your mama, she has a good heart!' And the fight was gone in a round of laughter and hugs."

So many of us have been taught to identify the expression of emotion with "emotionalism," with something undesirable, with something that is vulgar or verging on being hysterical. We forget that emotion is of the essence in human life. It is the propelling force that leads us, that stirs us to bring out the highest and finest in us, that makes us one with others and unique in ourselves. We forget, too, that emotion cannot be done away with no matter how much it is denied. If it doesn't come out one way, it will come out another. If we claim or pretend that we are not disturbed or angry, as example, and hold in for dear life, the anger will assuredly pop out elsewhere.

"You mean," exclaimed one man, horrified, "that we're supposed to show a child when we're angry? But that's just what you've been preaching to us *not* to do. . . ."

"That's the reason we've been reading this book. So we wouldn't have to get angry and spank a child on every occasion!" another put in.

No indeed! What we are thinking of at this point means something quite different. It does not mean that we should let out a continuous flood of anger in disciplining our children. That's not the point. The point is this:

> We need to avoid PILING UP
> ANGER inside ourselves.

When we pile up anger or resentment against *anybody* or *anything*, it is apt to erupt when we discipline a child. Little though we are aware of it, this happens with astonishing frequency. There's a good reason for it, although not a very

255

pretty reason, and one that is rather hard to own up to unless we are very honest and straight with ourselves. The reason is that *we dare to be ourselves with our children when we often do not dare to be ourselves with adults.* Our children have to take us willy-nilly; other people can take us or leave us as they choose. And so, unwittingly, we hold in and "behave ourselves" as it were with others, and then—poof, like a swirl of dust lifted suddenly by the wind—we let go on our child.

But still, the answer is not to deny anger. Nor is it to let anger out anywhere and everywhere. Neither offers any solution.

When we feel anger we,
too, need to
ADMIT it
and
RELEASE it
in unhurtful ways.

Just as we have tried to help our children admit and release and rechannel their negative feelings, so do we also need to try to help ourselves.

WE WERE ONCE LITTLE

"Mother," says Emmy, five, "you look so cross, don't you think you ought to paint a little bit?" Emmy has learned to paint out her feelings, so why shouldn't her mother?

In other words, Emmy is saying that what's sauce for the gosling is sauce for the goose, and the gander for that matter, too.

Grownups, in the same way as children, have let out all sorts of feelings in painting, in writing, or through acting or talking them out . . .

Several mothers bring what they have written or painted into a session of the mothers' group which they attend. One
256

mother had previously held in her upset feelings until they would burst bounds and she would lash out at her child. But now she was owning up to how she felt. "I get so mad at her," she said, "and I'm admitting it. When I feel it creeping up on me, instead of bursting out at her, I've been writing out how I feel."

She read a sample:

> She gets on my nerves. My furniture is all scratched, my walls have kick-marks on them. My stove is scratched, my refrigerator is scratched. My yard looks like a pigpen.
>
> I go crazy when she says no she won't let me wash her hair. I get irritated when I see her hopping on one leg and then on another when she has to go to the toilet. It annoys me when she insists on pawing the baby. I told her she could take her doll and pretend that it is her baby. But no, she wants the real thing. So then I say her feelings back to her, "You want the real baby" and then she goes and kicks the doll and calls it mommie. But meanwhile I'm angry most of the time.

"It sounds awful," she laughed, half apologetic. "But I'd rather it sounded awful on paper than on her poor little behind. And I do find that after I write it out I feel much calmer and don't have to whack at her any more."

As she went on working with the group, this mother discovered that her "fussiness" and tenseness about "the state of the house and yard" were exaggerated. They were reflections of her own mother's "fussiness" and tension. "As a child I had to keep things just right. I hated it. She was so particular. I hated her, I guess. And now I seem to want to do the same thing to my child. To get even, sort of. I can see it now, the madness hasn't been only at her."

Said another mother, "When I was little, my mother used to criticize me. I wasn't aware of it then, but I see now that in my unconscious I was really angry. Now, if any criticism comes from anybody I fill up with fury and I'm apt to let

257

out on my children. Only lately I've made up my mind that I'd find some other way."

She went on to recount how a note had come from school suggesting that she needed to have her older child's teeth cleaned. This she took as criticism and felt herself getting more and more upset. "I started snapping at both the children. And then I made myself stop. But I didn't try to hide how I felt. 'I'm mad,' I said to them, 'but not at you. So I don't want to take it out on you. You run on now and let me work it out by myself.'

" 'Don't you want to talk about it?' the girl asked sympathetically, while the boy ran and got me paper and chalk. 'Here, Mom, you can draw it.'

"I thanked them both and said I thought I would draw it. Well, I sat there a while in a daze, sort of. This couldn't mean me. I know now I didn't give my children all the love they needed in the first part of their lives. I've been making up for that lately. But I never neglected their care in the health way. They'd been to the dentist, in fact, just a week before. . . . I saw black and the blood raced to my head. I wanted to tear that school nurse from limb to limb. I felt quivering and shaking inside. I started to get dressed and found myself walking in circles. So I sat down again with one sock on and one sock off and I drew this picture. . . ."

Her picture was a mass of black blotches and angry zigzag lines with red angry streaks here and there, the blackness growing lighter as she progressed across the paper until at the final edge she changed from black to a clear, quiet blue.

"I felt better there, relaxed and calmer." She described how she had been. "Really relaxed and as calm as a lake of blue water. I thought, 'Now I can handle things better.' "

"How's it, Mom?" asked her girl a little while later.

"All okay again, darling."

"You got all the mad out."

In talking the incident over in the group, this mother also

came to realize that she had overreacted in terms of little-child feelings which she still carried in her. "When I thought of the school nurse, I was seeing my mother in my mind's eye and still listening with child ears to her critical voice."

A third mother in the group uttered constant complaints about her child, how he got on her nerves, how she flared up at him. Then one day her tongue slipped. She said something her conscious mind had never thought pertinent until it came out now. "He reminds me so of my father." After that she brought in a painting of how she had felt about her father when she was a child. Because of his cruelty to her she had wished him dead. As a result, she had drawn him in a coffin . . . "It makes me feel terrible to know that I had such terrible feelings toward him. But since I've talked about them here and have drawn them out, I feel so much kinder and I'm acting so much sweeter to my child."

In school a teacher who found herself getting impatient with the children when they made any noise discovered herself glancing constantly at the door to see if the principal were coming in. "I had such perpetual fear of her snooping." So instead of continuing to get irritable and impatient with her class, she drew a picture: A little girl was sitting stiffly and primly on a chair, very apparently in fear of moving to right or left. Near her a venomous-looking woman was standing behind a door, her ear plastered to it. "Listening to hear if I was doing something wrong . . . She was always snooping, my mother. Always listening. I had to be mousy-quiet for fear of her calling my father to come and whip me. . . ."

Although grown up and nearly forty, this woman was still letting out on the children the resentment to her mother that she had accumulated from her childhood years. "Drawing the picture helped me! But it helped me even more to bring it to you and to tell you about it; to have you listen acceptantly and not throw up your hands."

As with our children, the need for ACCEPTANCE applies to

us. We were all of us once little. We all had certain wants and needs that were not completely satisfied. Perhaps we remember, perhaps we do not. For, as we grow, we block many things out of consciousness that still live on in our unconscious minds. Our emotional hunger, our hurts, our fears, our childhood anger and resentments are among those things which we commonly block out. As a result, the hurts and fears and the resentments have piled up and we use our children, all unconsciously but literally, as whipping boys. Or we put on false faces through which they nevertheless feel the true state of our feelings.

Obviously, we cannot get at what we are not conscious of without professional help. If our hurts or fears or angry feelings are like big storms or hurricanes that rage perpetually and we try the home remedies without success, then we do well to seek professional help, suspecting that unconscious propulsions lie beneath the surface.

But if the hurts or fears or angry feelings are infrequent and small, like flurries of leaves in the wind, then the measures which we have been considering may prove effective. Our approach is to own up as much as possible to present-tense feelings as we are aware of them and to get them out. And, last but not least, to share them with an acceptant person.

Husbands and wives can do much for each other if they learn to be good listeners rather than ardent condemners. Where there is basic love and understanding, the acceptant attitude is easy to cultivate. The main thing is to take leave of the old precept that for "their own sake" we must criticize those whom we love.

Our children, too, may prove good "accepters"—far better ones than we've anticipated—if we've shown them how good it feels to have us accept them and if we give them a chance to accept us by bringing out our feelings to them for what they are. "I'm angry at you." . . . "I don't like what you're doing." . . . "When you act like that, you make me mad." Such a
260

downright avowal is far better than the confusing ambiguity of the pleasant voice worn with an angry scowl. More often than we anticipate, we find our children curiously acceptant after we have shown our willingness to accept their feelings for a period of time.

"I know how you feel, Mom," says six-year-old Toby. "Like rocks bumping up against all your insides!" . . . "I know how it is, Mom," says fifteen-year-old Ellie. "As if a thick shade were covering heaven and you couldn't see the sky or the sun!" . . . "Don't worry, Pop," says ten-year-old Peter. "There's nothing wrong with you really; just some cramps in the upper story . . . I get them sometimes."

If we have lost our tempers, as all of us do on occasion, if we have spanked and feel horrible, hangdog shame after, miserable that we've been such utter brutes, we need not defend ourselves forever and ever. We need not insist to ourselves, "Now I was justified" . . . We need not assert to our child, "If you hadn't acted that way I wouldn't have had to do what I did." We can be more honest. We can *share* our feelings. "I'm sorry, Buster. I could kick myself for losing my temper" . . . "I'm mad at myself now, for having gotten so mad at you."

As we do such sharing of ourselves with our children, a companionable mutuality grows. A deepening confidence. A sense that we and they have much in common. The humility and dignity of being human. A kind of oneness that cuts across the difference in the years between us and makes us akin.

WHEN PARENTS DIFFER

One of the most difficult kinds of feeling to own up to frankly to our children is that engendered when we differ with a husband or wife. Shades of old precepts rise and shake warning fingers at us: Don't let your child see any quarrels . . . He should never hear conflict between his parents . . . Keep a peaceful and united front. . . .

All this is fine provided that there are no quarrels or conflicts and that the peaceful and united front is real. But if it's counterfeit, then the same objections enter as when we camouflage with other sorts of feelings. Again our children sense the hypocrisy, they sense the real attitudes that exist.

"Grown-ups are so funny. They think children can't understand."

Over and over again parents claim that their children never witness any differences between them. Over and over again the children give evidence that they do.

"My father and mother begin yelling at each other every night as soon as I'm in bed," announced one youngster. When asked if he heard what they said, he answered, "Oh no. They yell in whispers. But it's all the same."

Delia is a very gentle, brooding five-year-old. Her father and mother claim that she has seen nothing of the war between them. But Delia gives away her secret worry in a painting. She puts a jumble of dots bunched and bumping together all over the paper in a confusion of color and design and then says:

> The girlie's crying
> Cause there's a war.
> Frogs and crickets and flies
> In a drop of water.
> Flies and crickets
> And mothers and fathers
> All in the war.

When we who are grown up look back we may perhaps remember our own childhood. If there was conflict between our parents we may recall our own discomfort even though everything was made to appear calm and serene. Yolande does. "My father would go around looking morose and my mother would look like a suffering angel. Then I'd know they had quarreled. I wanted to jump up and down and shout, 'Why don't you explode at each other? Why don't you throw things? Anything would be better than this awful stony quietness.' They thought I couldn't tell that anything was wrong. But I could . . . Then I'd feel that because they were hiding what was happening I had to hide that I knew. And so it took us further and further apart."

In contrast, the picture of the openness in Maria's family flashes back to us. In terms of our varying backgrounds, however, our own openness may be quite differently shaped. There is not just one single way but many ways of being frank and honest and sincere and of letting our children in on how we are really feeling. Some people show how they feel with volatile, swiftly shifting reactions. Others can let a child in better and more comfortably with more tempered words.

Said four-year-old Sandy's mother, sniffling, "Daddy and

I got mad at each other and we had a fight and now I'm crying. . . ."

"Uh-huh!" nodded Sandy sympathizing. "But soon you'll get over it and you'll be all right."

Sandy knew what fighting was and what crying was and that he himself got mad. So there was really nothing to worry about, especially since mother had confidence enough in him to let him in.

Olive, twelve, rushing into the house after playing with her friends one evening came upon her mother and father in a violent argument. She stopped and stared.

"Run along, Olive," her father said testily. "Can't you see we're fighting?"

"Okay," said Olive, "I'll let you finish in peace."

She knew from past experiences that her mother and father did have occasional squabbles, that they fought it out and got over it, just as she and her friends fought things out. They didn't want to be interfered with by children any more than children cared to have grownups interfere.

When we who are parents differ with each other, as all people differ at times, we do need privacy in which to battle things out. The point isn't that a child has to witness all. The point isn't that we need to explain on and on about the gory details or let him in on the various why's and what's and wherefore's. The important point is that we admit our differences. We need to be downright and open about the fact that we have moments in which we feel "mean" and angry toward each other. Then, as children see that we work things through, as they see that peace is renewed after a storm, their confidence grows. They come to understand that all human beings are human, that no vital companionship is insipid milk toast and honey, that there is struggle and clash in every human relationship and that this is *not apart from* but rather *a part of* loving. They come to know that differences can be taken openly in stride and that they can be worked through.

264

These things contribute to a wholesome, vigorous knowledge that their own differences can also be worked through—now, while they are children, with their parents, their sisters, their brothers, their friends; and later, when they grow up, with their own husbands and wives.

Several questions invariably arise in this place. "What," you ask, "are we supposed to do then when we don't agree about disciplining a child? Aren't fathers and mothers supposed to be consistent? Aren't they supposed always to be in accord with what the other one does?"

If they are in accord, so much the better. If they can think the same way and feel the same and agree basically on the mode and manner and principles of discipline—fine. This is certainly to be desired. If they can work through their ideas and their basic differences to the place where they really do feel the same way about bringing up their children, they do a very sound and important thing. But again, as in all relationships, there will be some differences that enter at times. And again, if there are differences, these are better approached frankly.

"Your father still believes in spanking. He makes me furious. I can't do a thing to educate him," said ten-year-old Chris's mother.

"I see, Mom," answered Chris, suddenly more comfortable because he was being let in on a secret which his parents had never actually hidden but about which they had obviously been trying to fool him. "I see, Mom," he repeated. "But honestly, Mom, it doesn't matter. Why don't you go your way and let him go his?"

Said Penny's father to his seven-year-old, "I get cross at mother when she gets cross at you." . . . Said her mother, "I get cross at daddy when he doesn't." Said Penny, serenely philosophic, "Well, different people have different hair and different noses. Why shouldn't they have different crossnesses, too?"

Many a husband still declares, "I always support my wife in the child's presence no matter whether I approve of what she does or not." But today this must be regarded as an outmoded policy.

"You know," Joyce, seventeen, was discussing discipline with her parents. "You guys made one big mistake."

"I know, now, we made many."

"But one especially. I'd get so furious when daddy would stand there biting the end of his pipe and avowing, 'Your mother is right.' He disliked you, Mom, for what you were doing. He disliked himself for being such a hypocrite. And he disliked me for being the cause.

"And anyway, as a child grows, he has to learn to adjust to different people's likes and dislikes. The important thing," she added with wisdom beyond her years, "is that no one asks him to do too much.

"As for you two. You haven't always agreed. Why should you? No two people ever do agree on every little thing every bit of the time, do they? Why put on an act? Why pretend? I like you both better since you've been yourselves."

We have heard over and over again that having a stable home to which he can belong is an important asset for a child's security. So it is. But conflict need not bespeak instability. The best of us have quarrels. The best of us work them through and come out stronger and with sturdier peace between us—not peace threatened by buried rumblings of war. The hidden undercurrents bring on the greater explosions when they erupt. They project themselves too readily onto children as substitute targets for husband or wife. If persistent conflict does exist even then it's better to be frank. Covering it up only makes it worse. Professional help may again be desirable to steer us in what we say. But when the breaks in peace are the natural breaks that come into any and every vigorous relationship, we can with freedom follow Joyce's precept. *Let's be ourselves!* Let's try to have our own
266

lives so ordered that we realize ourselves as fully and richly as we can as we move through our days.

MEETING OUR NEEDS

We have seen that in our children the hurts and fears and resentments mount as the basic and deep emotional satisfactions are lacking. Just so with us. No matter what age we are, as we said way back in the beginning, whether we are two months old or two years, thirteen or thirty—every human being needs certain emotional foodstuffs. He needs *affection*. He needs a sense of *belonging* and *being wanted*. He needs the lift of pleasure that comes through his senses. He needs the zest of *achievement* and the relish of *appreciation* from others for what he does. And, above all, he needs *acceptance* and *understanding*, the secure knowledge that some one person accepts him essentially when he is himself without pretense or sham.

Obviously, none of these satisfactions will pervade life in an uninterrupted stream. There will be breaks in all of them. They won't be present all the time. The idea is that we have some of each and in sufficient quantity to give us a modicum of inner peace.

These values come to different people in many different ways. The achievement of digging the soil and planting a garden and seeing flowers burst into bloom gives one person a sense of fulfillment. The achievement of working out a mathematical problem brings a similar lift to another. Participating in church or club activities may bring the feel of belongingness to one person. Going on a picnic and sharing the mountains and trees and the sky with a good companion may bring the same sort of satisfaction to another. Small activities throughout the days and weeks and years mount up so that the measure of their meaning grows as does the meaning of a warm handclasp between two friends.

The more we can accept ourselves, the more do others accept us. The less we need to hide from ourselves, the more free and open and generous we can be with others. The more loving we are, the more love comes to us. The more appreciative we are of others' feelings, the more acceptant and understanding, the more do these same values come to us.

We do best as we ask of ourselves. "Am I giving love and affection to others? Am I showing them appreciation? Am I accepting others with warm understanding, not criticizing or blaming but taking them as they are? Am I offering of myself and what is inside me? Am I contributing? Am I drawing from that creative spark which each of us possesses? Am I shaping something with hands or head or heart to share?"

For one truth stands above all others: We get as we give.

"Oh boy! This is the life!"

Index

Cruelty, 67, 114, 226, 229, 259
  to animals, 35–36, 48, 124
  to other children, 48, 71, 124, 180
    (*See also* Rivalry, sibling)
Crying, 41–42, 240
  of babies, 89–90
    as means of communication, 90–94
Cuddling, of babies, 90, 115
  in later development, 85, 116–118, 166

D

Daydreaming, 215
Deceit, 246
  (*See also* Lying)
Defiance, 230
  during adolescence, 139, 143
    (*See also* Rebelliousness)
Delinquency (*see* Juvenile delinquency)
Demands for attention (*see* Showing off)
Destructiveness, 30, 46, 48, 50, 52, 57–58, 168, 215, 217, 228
Diet, well-balanced, 96
Dirtiness (*see* Messiness)
Discipline, through activities, 7–8, 159–213
  definition of, 5
  failure of, 5–6
  first steps in, 18
  mechanical *vs.* instinctive, 235–237
  by negation, 56, 108–111, 223
  preventive, 7, 11–29, 158
  professional help in, 49–50, 125, 183, 247–248

Discipline, props in, 248
  rules for, 18, 25, 55–56, 156–158
  school, 1, 4, 51–52, 219–231
  stress periods in, 6
  time consumed in, 247
    (*See also* kinds of discipline, as Spanking)
Discontent (*see* Complaining)
Disobedience, 35, 37
  during adolescence, 140–141, 157
    (*See also* Behavior, bad)
Dispositions, good, through shared fun, 98
Disrespect, 69, 75
  during adolescence, 140
Distrust, 44–45
Doctors and childhood fears, 211–213
Dogs, 41–44
Dolls, 126, 213
Drawing, as release of feelings, 166–167, 258–259
  in school, 219
    (*See also* Painting; Pictures)
Dress self, refusal to (*see* Negativism)
Dressing up, as release of feelings, 203

E

Eating, 87
  and anger, 37, 43–44, 55–56, 97
  and fun, 95, 98
  good habits in, 97
  preferences in, 96
  voluntary, 112
    (*See also* Appetites)

P

Pacifiers, 102
Pain, results of, 211–213
Painting to release feelings, 191–193, 263
  by adults, 256–259
  in school, 219, 224–228
  supplies for, 193
Parent education classes, 205
Parents, and child's independence, 137–147
  as the child's world, 114
  mirroring of feelings by, 26–28, 40–45, 53, 55–57, 62, 106, 110–112, 117, 122–123, 128–129, 133–135, 142, 146, 149, 151, 154–155, 157, 167–168, 176–178, 180–183, 192–194, 203–205, 208–209
  quarreling, 210–211
  sharing of, 161
  study of child by, 22–29
Petting, by adolescents, 155–156
Physical development, 151
Physical ills (*see* Psychosomatic problems)
Pictures, 231, 250–251
  as means of communication, 189
  to release feelings, 189–195
  by adults, 258–259
  in school, 219, 224–228
Pinching, 126, 128, 130, 253
Play, 7, 158
  (*See also* Activities)
Poems, written by children, as release of feelings, 176–180, 183, 192, 253, 263
  kept by parents, 186–187

Poems, written by children, in school, 184–186, 222
Practicing, 16–17
Praise, 66
Pregnancy, fear of, 171
Prejudice, 230
  reasons for, 38, 57, 140
  (*See also* Intolerance)
Problem children, 238–239
Problem parents, 240
Psychodramas of family life, 205
Psychological development, 149
Psychological help, in discipline, 15, 49–50, 125, 183, 247–248
  for adults, 248
Psychosomatic problems, asthma, 57, 180–183
  coughing, 57, 78, 124, 183
  fatness, 148
  hay fever, 57
  hives, 57
  skin eruptions, 36
  tics, 49–50
Puberty, 151
Punishment, 37, 60, 66, 143, 228, 231, 242–243, 248
  hypocritical, 67
  by isolation, 22–23, 63, 67–68, 215
  by putting in corner, 69
  vs. reasoning, 68–71, 77
  resentment against, 67
  sincerity in, 68
  by spanking, 1–3, 67, 209–210, 237, 257, 265
  threat of, 69–70, 77
  by word, 5, 77
Puppet plays, as release of feelings, 207, 226
Puppets, paper-doll, 226

Q

Quarreling, 131, 139
 among husbands and wives,
  206, 254–255, 261–263
 admission of, 264–266
 about discipline of children,
  265–266
 surreptitious, 210–211, 262–
  263
 as part of loving, 243, 264
 (*See also* Fighting)

R

Radio programs, influence of, 199
Rape, 230
Reading problems, reasons for,
 224
Reasoning with child, 68–70, 248
Rebelliousness, 78–79, 139–140,
 142
 (*See also* Defiance)
Recognition, of achievements, 14,
 267–268
 of capabilities, 14
 (*See also* Appreciation)
Refusal-pattern, 75
 (*See also* Negativism)
Repentance, 245
Repression, 39–43
Resentment, 15, 34–35, 48, 267
 disguises of, 37–38, 123–127
 hidden, 34–35, 37–38, 49, 106,
  119–120, 122, 143, 215–
  216, 247–248
 and love, 243
 against new baby, 121–130,
  180
 against punishment, 67
 release of, 242, 255
  through acting, 203–205

Resentment, release of, through
 violence, 168, 170, 215
 sibling, 224–225
 against strictness, 156, 215
Respect for parents, lack of, 69,
 75
"Retarded" children, 225–228
Rewards, 63–65, 228, 248
 (*See also* Bribes)
Rhythms, natural, of infants, 107,
 113
 patterns in, 107
Rivalry in family life, naturalness
 of, 136
 with new baby, 119–130
 with parents, 135–136, 164
 sibling, 130–134
 rechanneling of, 131, 133–
  134
 (*See also* Jealousy)
Rocking, 93
Rowdiness, 143–144
Rudeness, 61
 during adolescence, 139–140
Rules and regulations, method of
 stating, 58–59
 natural resentment against, 59–
  60, 108–112
 necessary, 111–112, 156, 158
 in school, 228, 231
 need for, 58
 (*See also* Discipline by negation)
Running away, 53–54, 245

S

School, causes of failure in, 218–
 219, 222
 discipline in, 1, 4, 51–52
 release of feelings in, 219–231
School problems, reading difficulties, 224

1796